Frequent Frauds Found in Governments and Not-For-Profits

By Lynda Dennis, Ph.D., CPA, CGFO

Notice to Readers

Frequent Frauds Found in Governments and Not-For-Profits is intended solely for use in continuing professional education and not as a reference. It does not represent an official position of the Association of International Certified Professional Accountants, and it is distributed with the understanding that the author and publisher are not rendering legal, accounting, or other professional services in the publication. This course is intended to be an overview of the topics discussed within, and the author has made every attempt to verify the completeness and accuracy of the information herein. However, neither the author nor publisher can guarantee the applicability of the information found herein. If legal advice or other expert assistance is required, the services of a competent professional should be sought.

You can qualify to earn free CPE through our pilot testing program.
If interested, please visit aicpa.org at http://apps.aicpa.org/secure/CPESurvey.aspx.

Course Code: **746431**
FFGN GS-0417-0A
Revised: **January 2017**

TABLE OF CONTENTS

Recent Developments

Users of this course material are encouraged to visit the AICPA website at www.aicpa.org/CPESupplements to access supplemental learning material reflecting recent developments that may be applicable to this course. The AICPA anticipates that supplemental materials will be made available on a quarterly basis. Also available on this site are links to the various "Standards Trackers" on the AICPA's Financial Reporting Center which include recent standard-setting activity in the areas of accounting and financial reporting, audit and attest, and compilation, review and preparation.

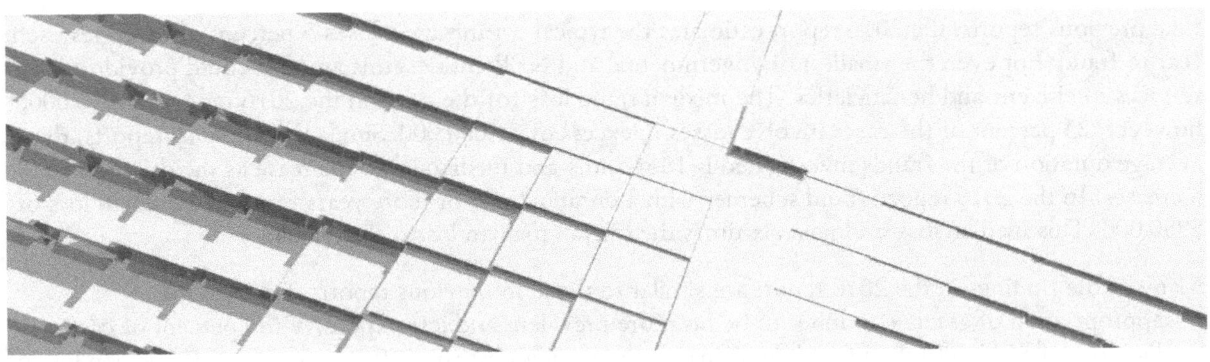

Overview

A ROADMAP FOR TODAY'S COURSE

Often those taking this course find it difficult to believe these fraud cases could actually occur. Auditors are also sometimes skeptical the situations presented would actually result in material financial statement fraud. On the other hand, others often believe any fraud is material when it occurs in governmental or not-for-profit (NFP) entities, as they most often involve public funds. Those working in government and NFP entities find the fraud cases in this course to be realistic.

2016 OCCUPATIONAL FRAUD REPORT

Every two years the Association of Certified Fraud Examiners releases a report based on cases of occupational fraud as reported by the certified fraud examiners investigating them. The 2016 *Report to the Nations on Occupational Fraud and Abuse* summarizes 2,410 fraud cases of which 1,038 (49 percent) relate to frauds in the United States, with governmental and public administration entities representing almost 11 percent of the victim organizations. Health care, education, religious, charitable, and social services entities represent 15 percent of the cases investigated. Although these and governmental entities represent some of the industries with the greatest frequency of fraud, the amounts of the fraud losses are not as large as those of other industries. Governmental entities report a median loss of $133,000, while health care, education, religious, charitable, and social services entities report median losses of $120,000; $62,000; and $82,000, respectively. Federal level governmental entities experience a median loss of $194,000, while states (or provinces) and local governmental entities report median losses of $100,000 and $80,000, respectively.

Like previous reports, the 2016 report estimates the typical organization loses 5 percent of revenues each year to fraud. For even the smallest of governmental and NFP entities, this amount could provide a lot of services to citizens and beneficiaries. The median fraud loss for the cases in the 2016 report is $150,000; however, 23 percent of the cases involve losses in excess of $1,000,000. Similar to previous reports, the average duration of the frauds investigated is 18 months and median losses increase as the duration increases. In the 2016 report, fraud schemes with a duration of 5 or more years result in a median loss of $850,000. This median loss is almost six times the overall median loss of $150,000.

Many of the findings in the 2016 report are similar to those in previous reports. For example, misappropriation of assets continues to be far more prevalent and less expensive (83 percent of cases, median loss of $125,000) than fraudulent financial reporting (less than 10 percent of cases, median loss of $975,000). In governmental, health care, education, religious, charitable, and social services entities, financial statement fraud is fairly infrequent, ranging from a frequency of 4 percent in religious, charitable, and social services entities to 13 percent in health care entities.

Once again, tips are the most common way frauds are detected, and employees provide approximately 52 percent of these tips. Fraud telephone hotlines are the most commonly used single method to report fraud (40 percent). When combined, tips reported using email (34 percent) and online forms (24 percent), however, are the most common method for reporting fraud.

Small organizations (fewer than 100 employees) and the largest organizations (more than 10,000 employees) report the same median loss in this report—$150,000. Common fraud schemes perpetrated on small organizations include billing fraud (27 percent), check tampering (20 percent), skimming (19 percent), and theft of noncash items (19 percent). In governmental and NFP entities, the most common misappropriation of assets fraud schemes are somewhat different. Common frauds found in these organizations are as follows:

	Governments	**Health Care Entities**	**Education**	**Religious, Charitable, and Social Services Entities**
Billing frauds	25%	31%	34%	25%
Theft of cash on hand	11%	11%	17%	14%
Check tampering	9%	15%	8%	25%
Skimming	14%	13%	25%	19%
Expense reimbursement	16%	20%	16%	25%

According to the 2016 report, the most effective internal controls reduce the median fraud loss by 1 percent to 54 percent, as well as the average duration of the fraud by 33 percent to 50 percent. Controls found to be effective in the cases investigated include the following:

- *Proactive data monitoring and analysis*. Median fraud losses with and without this control are $92,000 and $200,000, respectively.
- *Surprise audits*. Median fraud losses with and without this control are $100,000 and $195,000, respectively.
- *Dedicated fraud department or team.* Median fraud losses with and without this control are $100,000 and $192,000, respectively.
- *Formal fraud risk assessments*. Median fraud losses with and without this control are $100,000 and $187,000, respectively.
- *Management review.* Median fraud losses with and without this control are $100,000 and $200,000, respectively.
- *Fraud hotlines*: Median fraud losses with and without this control are $100,000 and $200,000, respectively.

Recent Frauds

Dixon, Illinois

One of the largest and most noteworthy misappropriation of assets fraud cases in years, made national news in 2012. In the small town of Dixon, Illinois, the long-term and highly respected comptroller, Rita Crundwell, was arrested in April 2012 and then later indicted by a federal grand jury for embezzling $53 million from the city over a period of 22 years. Ms. Crundwell pleaded guilty to the charges in November 2012 and was sentenced to 19.5 years in federal prison on February 2013 on a single count of wire fraud.

This fraud scheme in Dixon, Illinois is a classic example of a fraud "perfect storm" as it includes the following:

- A long-term and trusted employee holding a high level position in the accounting and finance function
- Little, if any, segregation of duties as Ms. Crundwell controlled almost everything involving the city's monies as early as 1983
- A "secret" bank account listing "RSCDA c/o Rita Crundwell" as the second account holder into which funds from the State of Illinois were diverted
- Bank statements for the "secret" account being sent to a post office box Ms. Crundwell controlled
- The perpetrator living an extremely lavish lifestyle including a multimillion-dollar horse breeding and showing empire
- Ms. Crundwell playing on the auditor's Softball team during the 1980s
- Fictitious invoices purported to be from the State of Illinois to show funds fraudulently deposited into the RSCDA "secret" account being used for legitimate purposes
- The current auditor resigning in 2006 from the audit of the city in order to perform only compilation services and then recommending another CPA firm to perform the audit of the city's financial statements

- Embezzlement of approximately $30 million (55 percent of the total amount misappropriated over the 22-year duration of the fraud scheme) over a 6-year period from 2006 through the identification of the fraud in late 2011
- Elected and appointed city officials being provided misleading information by Ms. Crundwell as to the city's financial status
- A commission form of government overseen by part-time commissioners where Ms. Crundwell educated newly elected officials on the operations of her office and the city in general

Like many fraud schemes, this fraud was discovered by the city clerk who was performing some of Ms. Crundwell's functions when she was out of town on one of her numerous horse competitions. A routine request for all bank statements resulted in the city clerk noticing the "secret" account which she brought to the attention of the Mayor who contacted the FBI. Over a five-month period, the FBI conducted an undercover investigation resulting in the arrest of Ms. Crundwell by the FBI on April 17, 2012.

The facts of this actual fraud emphasize how important it is for the auditor to exercise professional skepticism when performing not only fraud-related procedures but throughout the entire audit process. Such professional skepticism begins with the client continuance or acceptance process and extends through the signing of the auditor's report on the financial statements. Although the cases in this course may appear unrealistic or immaterial in nature, it is important to remember that many frauds start small and grow into material amounts. In fact, in the first year of the Dixon, Illinois fraud, Ms. Crundwell embezzled the relatively small amount of $181,000.

American Legacy Foundation

Founded in 1999 out of the Master Settlement Agreement with cigarette companies and located in Washington D.C., the American Legacy Foundation's annual revenues exceed $320 million. Unfortunately, the foundation was not able to handle this much cash in its early frenetic days. Little oversight was exercised over financial transactions and few controls were in place during this time.

Deen Sanwoola, the foundation's sixth hire in October 1999, was given responsibility for building the foundation's IT department. No one realized in the early days that the IT department did not have adequate financial controls. For example, Sanwoola was responsible for ordering electronic equipment, logging it as being received, and ensuring it was in place.

Soon after his arrival, Sanwoola began buying various pieces of IT equipment and software packages, purchasing much of the equipment from a single company in suburban Maryland. His first questionable purchase, occurring in December 1999, was $18,000 of computer related equipment with an estimated retail value of $7,000. Questionable purchases of various types of computer equipment continued over the next several years peaking in 2006 with 49 purchases. In some cases, the foundation has paid far more for items than their worth and in other cases has paid inflated prices for equipment they never received.

Over his tenure, Sanwoola likely generated upwards of 255 invoices for computer equipment approximately 75 percent of which the foundation believes to be fraudulent. During his time with the foundation (1999–2007), Sanwoola and the foundation's CFO became close friends. Like many fraudsters, everyone loved Sanwoola and all were very surprised in early 2007 upon his announcement that he would be leaving to move to Nigeria.

Six months after Sanwoola's departure, an executive at the foundation could not locate computer equipment listed on the inventory. He informed the foundation's CFO of the situation who did not take the complaint seriously and did not initiate an investigation. Three years later, this same executive, bypassing the CFO, informed the CEO of another similar situation. The foundation quickly hired forensic examiners to investigate and the CEO notified the board. Early in the forensic investigation, the examiners noted an organization with the size and breadth of the foundation would not have any need to spend as much as they did on information technology.

Using recovered files from a backup computer server in Chicago, forensic examiners found a template for invoices from the Maryland computer supply company. In addition, the examiners found computer code showing the template had been designed and generated by someone using Sanwoola's log-in credentials. As a result of the forensic examination, foundation officials concluded $3.4 million of the $4.5 million in checks and credit card charges associated with the Maryland company were fraudulent.

Questionable invoices paid by the foundation allegedly came from a defunct Maryland company, Xclusiv; however, some questionable invoices spelled the name of the company slightly differently (Xclusive). Corporate directors for Xclusiv claim not to know Sanwoola and one claims to never have heard of the foundation. According to this director, Xclusiv was a barbershop and not a computer supply company.

Another director of Xclusiv claims the company did sell computers to the foundation but he is unsure how many or who arranged it. Additionally, this director speculates identify theft is the reason his name and Social Security number ended up on recovered foundation documents. This director also asserts his brother likely sold Sanwoola a house in the Greenbelt, even though property records indicate the seller's name is the same name as the director.

Like the Dixon, Illinois fraud, the facts of this actual fraud also emphasize how important it is for the auditor to exercise professional skepticism. For example, when performing non fraud-related procedures, the auditors in this case might have performed procedures to determine the validity of vendors as part of detail tests of disbursements or the purchasing cycle. This fraud did not come to the attention of management until several years after the fraudster left the employ of the foundation. In hindsight, it seems the auditor might have responded to the fraud risk resulting from the missing and ineffective controls by expanding the nature, timing, and extent of the planned further audit procedures.

Chapter 1

Case 1: Interim Financial Reporting

Learning Objectives

After completing this chapter, you should be able to do the following:

- Determine relevant fraud risks relating to management override in a fictitious government.
- Identify circumstances in a fictitious government, which might also be present in an actual government, that could increase fraud risks in a governmental organization.

Before We Start

This case involves compliance with bond covenants and reporting required information to rating agencies, trustees, and other oversight entities. Because noncompliance with bond covenants could have a material effect on a government's financial statements, it may be considered a significant risk area. Additionally, the potential for management to override existing controls to manipulate financial and operational information to be in compliance with bond covenants might lead the auditor to identify this as a fraud risk area.

Management override is an area of concern for auditors because management may be able to easily access data and systems. In addition, employees may be reluctant to discuss management abuses during the auditor's fraud inquiry procedures. Management override most often occurs in the following areas:

- Journal entries
- Estimates

- Business rationale for transactions
  - Bribes and kickbacks
  - Billing schemes

Professional standards require the auditor to assess the risk of material misstatement due to fraud using the components of the fraud triangle. It is not necessary for all of the following fraud risks to be present for the auditor to conclude there is a specific risk of material misstatement due to fraud:

- Opportunity
- Incentive or pressure (real or perceived)
- Rationalization or attitude

In all areas of the audit, the auditor is required to exercise professional skepticism, which is an attitude requiring the auditor to have a questioning mind and to critically assess audit evidence. The characteristics of skepticism may help auditors better understand this concept of professional skepticism.

Characteristics of skepticism are as follows:

- Questioning mind. Be disposed to inquiry with some sense of doubt.
- Suspension of judgment. Do not pass judgment until appropriate evidence is obtained.
- Search for knowledge. Investigate beyond the obvious with a desire to corroborate.
- Interpersonal understanding. Motivations and perceptions can lead to biased or misleading information (or both).
- Autonomy. Maintain self-direction, moral independence, and the conviction to decide for oneself.
- Self-esteem. Maintain self-confidence to resist persuasion and to challenge assumptions.

Knowledge Check

1. Which is NOT an area in which management override may occur?

    a. Billing schemes.
    b. Journal entries.
    c. Estimates.
    d. Price fixing between two vendors.

Background

Balsa Wood County[1] is a full service, medium-sized county in the south. The county provides a number of services to the cities within its boundaries through various interlocal agreements. All cities use the County Tax Assessor and Collector to assess and collect their municipal taxes. The county remits collections, net of a two percent administrative charge, to the cities bi-weekly during peak collection periods (such as the first six months after taxes are levied) and monthly during non-peak collection

[1] All organization names used in this course are purely fictitious as are the individuals depicted therein. Any similarity to real organizations or persons is purely coincidental.

periods. Some cities contract with the county to provide public safety services and the county bills for these services monthly.

Balsa Wood grew slowly until the mid-1950s when oil was discovered near its county seat. The county experienced a significant amount of consistent growth until the mid-1980s. Growth in the state virtually halted in the late 1980s and did not resume until the mid-1990s. Unfortunately for Balsa Wood County, the economic resurgence of the 1990s benefited the surrounding counties and those along the coast rather than Balsa Wood. The state and Balsa Wood County also experienced a significant economic downturn during the "Great Recession" of the late 2000s.

In an effort to compete with the surrounding areas for economic growth, Balsa Wood voters approved a $50,000,000 general obligation bond issue in the late 1990s. As part of the referendum, the voters approved an annual millage rate of 1.5 mills for debt service on the bonds. Growth and development projections prepared by the county's consultants indicated the additional 1.5 mills would be adequate to meet the annual debt service requirements.

Proceeds of the bonds were used to fund road improvements and to build a minor league baseball stadium, both in an attempt to attract economic investment in the county. Unfortunately, the county lost its bid for a minor league baseball expansion team and the stadium facility is used mainly for area concerts and high school sporting events. Very little economic or population growth has occurred in the county since it issued the general obligation bonds. The county's population has remained stable in total with more residents moving from the smaller cities in the rural portions of the county to the county seat rather than to neighboring counties.

Knowledge Check

2. Which is accurate of Balsa Wood County?

   a. Balsa Wood County is a full service, medium-sized county.
   b. The county provides no services to the cities within its boundaries through various interlocal agreements.
   c. Balsa Wood grew quickly until the mid-1950s.
   d. Balsa Wood issued bonds to construct a new water treatment facility.

3. Which is accurate of Balsa Wood County?

   a. The county remits collections, net of a two percent administrative charge, to the cities bi-weekly during peak collection periods (such as the first six months after taxes are levied) and monthly during non-peak collection periods.
   b. A few cities use the county tax assessor and collector to assess and collect their municipal taxes.
   c. Growth in the state accelerated in the late 1970s.
   d. The county has not needed to increase tax rates in recent years.

4. Which is accurate of Balsa Wood County?

   a. The stadium facility is used mainly for area concerts and high school sporting events.
   b. The current county manager convinced the county commission to build the baseball stadium.
   c. The county has recently been awarded a minor league baseball expansion team.
   d. The county is on the verge of declaring bankruptcy under Chapter 7.

The county and the trustee for the bonds entered into a number of covenants with respect to the general obligation bonds. Should any of the covenants be violated, the bonds may be called by the trustee. Specific relevant covenants are illustrated in the following list:

Balsa Wood County **General Obligation Bond Covenants**
Annual assessment of the voter-approved 1.5 mills for debt service requirements.
Imposition of additional *ad valorem* taxes should taxes from the 1.5 mills be insufficient to meet annual debt service requirements.
Any taxes generated by the 1.5 mills in excess of annual debt service requirements are required to be deposited into an interest and sinking fund for early retirement of the bonds.
Maintenance of an average annual *ad valorem* tax collection rate of 95 percent.
Maintenance of a cumulative *ad valorem* tax collection rate of 80 percent in the first two quarters after the tax levy.
Adequate property insurance covering the replacement value of the stadium.
Proper maintenance of the baseball stadium facility and equipment.
Tri-annual appraisals of the baseball stadium facility and equipment.
Annual audited financial statements prepared on the GAAP basis.
Quarterly reporting including quarter and year-to-date • budget-based financial statements for the general and water and sewer funds; • tax levies and collections; • certificate of insurance for the baseball stadium facility and equipment; and, • amounts spent to maintain the baseball stadium facility and equipment.

For the past four years, the county needed to increase its operating millage rate to provide sufficient funds to meet the annual debt service requirements on the general obligation bonds. However, the county chose to use accumulated unrestricted fund balance amounts to "balance its budget" in lieu of raising property taxes or reducing services.

The Case

The following exchange occurs after the first quarter of the fiscal year between the county manager, Diane Young, and the finance director, Robert Evans.

"Diane, I wanted to let you know I finished the annual and first quarter bond reporting package last night. We barely complied with our covenants last year and the first quarter does not look good. I am not sure we are going to meet the 80 percent ad valorem collection covenant next quarter. I know this is not good news but I wanted you to be aware of the situation."

"Thanks, Robert. I certainly appreciate the heads up on this. As you know, the commission is looking for something else to blame on me and I am not sure how much longer I will have a job here. Violating our bond covenants might be the excuse they need to get rid of me."

"That would be a real shame, Diane. I don't see how they can blame you for their mistakes. You were not even here when we built that white elephant baseball stadium and the roads that lead to nowhere. I guess they don't give you any credit for the parks and recreation programs you created to keep people from leaving the county."

"You and I know this but we also know a county manager is only as good as his or her last fiscal year. Things might work out for me if I can convince the big box store developer to build here. They are supposed to be making their decision sometime in the next several months. Hopefully, we won't violate any bond covenants between now and then. I don't think anyone would want to invest in a county that can't even pay its bills!"

"I, and a lot of others around here, think you are doing a great job considering the mess you inherited from our last county manager. Hopefully, things will work out with the big box people. I'll certainly do everything I can to help you keep your job."

During the next few months, Robert monitors maintenance expenditures for the stadium and tax collections to make sure the county will meet its covenants.

Expenditures for maintenance of the stadium were delayed due to the medical leave of absence taken by the public works director. Even though the county is evaluated annually as to its stadium maintenance covenant, Robert does not want to take any chances in the interim.

Robert calls the public works superintendent, Ken Alda, to solicit his help.

"Hey Ken, this is Robert Evans over in finance. I'm working on something here and was wondering if you could help me with it."

"I'll try Robert. What do you need?"

"I know the painting of the stadium locker rooms is scheduled for the fourth quarter when the use is minimal. However, I need to show the analysts in New York we are spending money on the stadium each quarter. With your boss being out on medical leave, we delayed a lot of maintenance at the stadium. Do you think you could process a purchase order for the painting this quarter?"

"Well, Robert, that's not really my area of expertise. The boss is real funny about the quality of the work we have done at the stadium. I would hate to do something he wouldn't like or approve. Besides, the place is booked almost every weekend now that the playoffs have started. It would be pretty difficult to get things painted with all those kids running in and out every week."

"Yeah, I know. I don't want to put you in a bad place but I am really looking for some help here. What if you process a purchase order but don't issue it? Then, after the quarterly reports are run, you can cancel it. This way, I'll get what I need to show the folks in New York and you won't be in trouble with your boss."

"You're the guy in charge of the numbers, if you say this will work, I don't have a problem with it. I'll take care of it this afternoon."

"Thanks a lot, Ken. I appreciate it."

At the end of the second quarter, Robert prepares the financial statements and other information required by the bond covenants. As he had suspected, the cumulative 80 percent tax collection rate was not achieved for the first two quarters. The county collected only 70 percent of its tax levy in the first two quarters. Robert is very concerned not only for the county manager's job but also for his own if he is unable to show the county has complied with its bond covenants.

Muttering to himself, Robert says "There has to be a way to get these collections up to 80 percent. What can I do.. .wait, let me see what we collected the first week of this quarter!"

Looking at the collections made during the first week of the third quarter, Robert finds the additional collections bring the cumulative collection rate to 75 percent.

Still muttering, he says "I can journal entry the subsequent collections into the second quarter and then reverse them in the third quarter for reporting to the trustee. That will get me close, but still no cigar. What else can I do?"

After taking a break to walk the halls, Robert pumps his fist and says "Yes! I know what to do" and runs back to his office. Pulling up the tax collection information for the cities in the county, Robert determines municipal collections during the last month of the second quarter were higher than in prior years. He also notes that taxes collected during the last two weeks of the second quarter have not yet been remitted to the cities.

After making a few calculations, Robert determines he can get the cumulative tax collection ratio to 81 percent by "borrowing" funds from the cities. Because of the higher than normal municipal collections, the cities will still receive an amount comparable to the same period in the prior year. He prepares journal entries to make the second and third quarter adjustments and reversals and also prepares the bank draft requests to transfer the adjusted amounts to the various cities. Using the adjusted second quarter information, he prepares the quarterly bond compliance reporting package and readies it for mailing.

The next morning Robert meets with the county manager to update her on the situation.

"Diane, I wanted you to know I completed the second quarter reports for the New York folks last night and everything worked out fine. I admit I was a little worried these last few months about the numbers but I managed to make things work. You are too good of an administrator to lose and I did not want to be responsible for you losing your job here."

"I doubt anyone would have blamed you if I lost my job, Robert. It is great to know that at least I don't have to worry about violating any bond covenants. Thanks for making my day!"

Knowledge Check

5. Which is accurate of Balsa Wood County?

    a. The county and the trustee for the bonds entered into two covenants with respect to the general obligation bonds.
    b. Should any of the covenants related to the general obligation bonds be violated, the bonds may be called by the trustee.
    c. The county is not required to have audited financial statements.
    d. The county manager manipulated property tax collections in the current year in order to meet bond covenants.

EXERCISES

1. Do any of the situations described in this case study represent fraud? If so, what situations and how did they occur?

2. What preliminary audit procedures might have detected this situation?

3. What other audit procedures might have detected this situation?

4. If you were the auditor and discovered this situation, would you communicate this situation to others? If so, to whom? How might this situation affect any planned reliance on internal controls?

Chapter 2

Case 2: Misappropriation of Benefits

Learning Objectives

After completing this chapter, you should be able to do the following:

- Determine how benefits might be misappropriated in a fictitious not-for-profit (NFP) entity.
- Use the fraud triangle in light of operations at offsite locations in a fictitious NFP.

Before We Start

Management and auditors may sometimes overlook fraud risks associated with benefit programs because there is typically no physical asset relating to the benefit. Program benefits provided by NFPs that may be provided to beneficiaries not qualifying for the benefit or not qualifying for the level of benefit provided include the following:

- Unemployment
- Food stamps
- Housing assistance
- Financial aid
- Health care
- Legal assistance
- Child care
- Membership

Program benefits might be misappropriated when the following indicators are present:

- Copies of missing application forms and underlying supporting documentation
- Participant files lacking required information (for example, interview sheets, tax returns, and so on)
- Decentralized intake centers or centralized intake centers with little or no monitoring by management or supervisory personnel
- Inadequately trained or supervised program personnel
- Inadequate or ineffective controls over program assets
- Lack of periodic physical inventories of program assets

BACKGROUND

Healthy Families is a large regional NFP organized under IRC Section 501(c)(3), controlling and operating 25 separately incorporated branch locations in a five-county area. The operating budget for all locations has averaged $30,000,000 over the past three years. Major sources of revenue for Healthy Families are membership dues (35 percent of operating revenues) and program fees (40 percent of operating revenues). Additionally, Healthy Families is a United Way agency and as such receives approximately $300,000 each year. For the current year, United Way funding is for three new after school and summer camp programs in low-income areas in two counties ($200,000) and for financial assistance to qualifying participants in after school and summer camp programs at any Healthy Families location ($100,000).

Oversight responsibility is performed by a centrally located administrative office. Branch operations range from providing minimal services off-site to providing a full range of services both on and off-site. Each branch is operated by a branch manager and each branch is staffed with at least one program coordinator and a full or part-time office manager.

Each branch manager hires and fires all personnel needed to operate the branch. The Board formally adopted a written Personnel Policy two years ago that included hiring and firing guidelines for branch managers. No formal compensation system exists at any level of the organization as the local economic circumstances of the various branch office locations dictate branch salaries. Administrative office personnel and branch managers are compensated commensurate with prevailing market rates for similar work. Mid-management, office support, and line personnel are paid less than the market which has resulted in high turnover rates throughout Healthy Families.

For the past 25 years, Healthy Families has employed a professional development director. The current development director was hired from a large out-of-state NFP 10 years ago. He is responsible for all grant writing, preparing the annual United Way funding request, and fundraising for all Healthy Families locations. To date, Healthy Families has had very little grant activity because staff does not want to be limited by grant provisions and procedures. At the direction of the development director, all branch personnel are directly involved in the annual fundraising appeal conducted each February.

Knowledge Check

1. Which is accurate of Healthy Families?

    a. Healthy Families receives 10 percent of operating revenues from program fees.
    b. Healthy Families is a United Way agency and as such receives approximately $300,000 each year.
    c. Healthy Families operates in a 10-county area.
    d. Healthy Families is heavily dependent on grant revenues to fund its programs.

2. Which is accurate of Healthy Families?

    a. Few branches are staffed with program coordinators.
    b. Healthy Families does not have any off site locations providing program services.
    c. Branch operations range from providing minimal services off-site to providing a full range of services both on and off-site.
    d. All branch operations are subject to significant oversight by administrative office executive leadership.

3. Which is accurate of Healthy Families?

    a. The board formally adopted a written personnel policy two years ago that included hiring and firing guidelines for branch managers.
    b. Branch managers cannot hire or fire personnel needed to operate the branch.
    c. Healthy Families does not have a formal written personnel policy.
    d. Few branch personnel are directly involved in the annual fundraising appeal.

4. Which is accurate of Healthy Families?

    a. Administrative office personnel and branch managers are not compensated commensurate with prevailing market rates for similar work.
    b. No formal compensation system exists at any level of the organization as the local economic circumstances of the various branch office locations dictate branch salaries.
    c. The annual fundraising appeal is conducted each January.
    d. Because of its significant grant funding, it is not necessary for Healthy Families to conduct an annual fundraising appeal.

5. Which is accurate of Healthy Families?

    a. Due to its minimal fundraising efforts, Healthy Families does not employ a full time development director.
    b. For the past 25 years, Healthy Families has employed a professional development director.
    c. Historically, Healthy Families has had a great deal of grant activity.
    d. The current development director was hired from a small NFP.

THE CASE

The following discussion takes place at the April all-staff meeting held at the administrative offices. Present at the meeting are the CEO, Jerry Bird; the two operating vice presidents, Kelly Nelson and John Carter; the CFO, Abby Brooks; the development director, Rob Strait; and all branch managers.

"All right, listen up everyone. As you know, we completed the annual campaign last month and Rob will now give us the final results."

"Thanks, Jerry. First, I want to thank all of you and your staff for working so hard to make this year's campaign such a success. It was touch-and-go the first few weeks but overall, I believe we were successful. Unfortunately, we were short of our goal by almost $500,000."

"Rob, what happened that caused us to be short of our goal? I thought we were on target and, frankly, I am surprised to hear we fell short."

"Well, John, one of the major reasons we fell short was because the Board fell short of their $750,000 goal by more than $200,000. We also had several branches that were unable to meet their goal and four of our perennial corporate sponsors decreased their level of sponsorship."

A lengthy discussion ensues among all present regarding the details of the successes and failures of the annual campaign.

"Jerry, I have a question."

"Go ahead, Abby."

"Regardless of who did or did not meet their campaign goals and why, we need to figure out how we are going to amend our budget for the $500,000 we did not raise. From where I am sitting, we will need to cut programs or staff or both to compensate for the shortfall."

"Abby, you are always so predictable. You are always crying how the sky is falling. Can we simply find the money somewhere else?"

"Well, Rob, we could do that but it will fall to you to make it happen. I am not comfortable expanding or continuing services based on 'future funding' which may or may not materialize. What programs will be most impacted if we have to cut services, John?"

"All you branch managers jump in and correct me if I'm wrong, but I think the two new teen weekend programs we had planned at the Park South and Downtown branches would be one of the first to go. We might also have to consider limiting the number of scholarships for summer day camp and Camp Tahoe this summer."

"Wait a minute, John, we are already taking applications for Camp Tahoe and the number of registrants needing financial assistance seems to be more than last year. What am I supposed to do, turn them away?"

"Hold on there, Scott. As the director of Camp Tahoe I expect you to try and find a solution instead of complaining."

CFO, Abby Brooks speaks up. "Hang on everyone. Now that I know what programs might need to be cut I have an idea. I was at a training session the other day and I heard Joe Durham from DHHS talking about some extra funding the state may have this spring for summer programs. Apparently, several of their grantees were unable to get some of their programs up and running and the state is looking to reallocate the funds before their yearend in June."

"I don't know, Abby, we have always tried to stay away from state or federal funding because of all the strings. Besides, you are always telling us we will have to do things differently if we get any grant funding."

"Well, Rob, we would possibly have to have a different kind of audit depending on how much we received and how much we spent. At this point, I would rather deal with the additional red tape than have to turn kids away from summer camp."

CEO, Jerry Bird looks at the group. "Here is what we need to do folks. Abby, you and Rob contact DHHS and get us first in line for those excess funds. Kelly, you and John figure out what programs could be cut or reduced in case the state money does not come our way. All you branch managers, get working on your donors and merchants to get us as many freebies and volunteers as you can so we won't have to buy as many supplies for our summer programs. Any money we don't have to spend on supplies and payroll can be used for scholarships. What are you waiting for people? We are adjourned!"

Later that afternoon Abby and Rob contact DHHS to determine if DHHS has any funding available for any programs like those offered by Healthy Families. The DHHS area manager, Rita Nichols, tells Abby and Rob their summer camp programs have the highest likelihood of being funded because they are the types of programs the original grantees were supposed to provide. She tells Abby and Rob to send a letter of interest and a detailed budget of the summer camp programs they would like to have funded to her as soon as possible.

Later Abby, John, Kelly, and Rob are in Abby's office.

"Thanks for helping me with these budgets and the letter of interest guys. I will overnight them to Rita on my way home today."

"I really hope we are able to get something out of the state guys. No one wants Jerry to have to tell the board we are cutting services."

"You got that right, Kelly. I don't care what kind of hoops the state makes us jump through as long as we get the funding. It seemed Rita was pretty receptive to looking at funding our summer programs."

"We all need to keep our fingers crossed Rita can find some funding for us."

A week later, DHHS informs Healthy Families they will receive $350,000 to provide financial assistance to qualified individuals wishing to attend summer camps. Due to a requirement in the original funding agreement between the state DHHS and the federal Department of Education, the grantee will be Healthy Families with the benefiting branches the sub recipients. Monies available under the grant will be disbursed directly to qualified recipients at the direction of the applicable branch.

To ensure qualified applicants reimburse Healthy Families for the financial assistance provided, DHHS will send the beneficiary checks (payable to the recipient) directly to the branch providing the actual financial assistance. Branch personnel will then ask beneficiaries to endorse the checks over to Healthy Families. Under the terms of the grant, each branch will weekly send DHHS a listing of that week's grant recipients. The state has agreed to process and mail financial assistance checks within 10 working days.

CFO, Abby Brooks, calls a meeting with all branch managers and the operating vice presidents to go over the procedures that will need to be followed.

"Okay, everyone, settle down. I know we are all relieved and excited about the state funding but I need you to focus on some details with me for the next 30 or so minutes. There are some pretty rigid requirements applicants need to meet in order to receive the financial assistance available under this grant. In your packets you will find a copy of the state application for financial assistance which..."

Abby spends the next few minutes going over the required procedures for determining qualified individuals and documentation requirements.

"Alright, let me see if I have this straight. No one receives assistance unless they are at 200 percent or below of the state poverty level. We need a copy of their last pay stub or a letter from their employer stating their current salary and withholdings. Then we ask all these questions, get their social security number, and have them sign the form."

"That is correct, Scott. Remember, the documentation is very important. Whoever is going to be processing the paperwork needs to be aware of how important it is to follow all the procedures. We do not want to have to give back any money to the state because we did not properly qualify someone or document everything we needed in the file."

"Maybe if I am lucky, I will get everything filled out in time for the kids to attend the camp closing ceremony!"

"Come on Scott, you can have someone else do this instead of you as long as you are comfortable with how well they understand the process and documentation requirements."

"What do you mean, Abby? Are you saying I could have my assistant or one of the counselors do all of this?"

"Anyone can do it, Scott, as long as they are trained in the proper procedures. You are too busy during the summer keeping things running, parents happy, and kids from getting snake bit to have to deal with this type of paperwork. Let someone else do it for you."

"What a great idea, Abby. I will."

Two weeks later Camp Tahoe director, Scott Campbell, is training his summer assistant, Kathy Larson.

"Okay Scott. I think I have it down now. It is still pretty amazing the state came through with funding for us this summer. Too bad they didn't make some of this available for raises. I barely got by on what you paid me last summer and this summer looks like things will be even tighter."

"I know I don't pay you nearly what you're worth but I make up for it by giving you all the candy bars and soda you want. Besides, the state money had to be split among us and the other branches. I tried to get all of it but that suggestion went over like a lead balloon at the all-staff meeting last month."

"I know you try, Scott, but candy bars don't pay the rent. I appreciate the thought though. What did you mean about having to share the state money with the other branches?"

"Oh, I thought I had told you. The state did not want all the money to be spent on just one camp so Jerry allocated it to all the branches using some kind of voodoo economics formula Abby came up with. That woman could find a way to allocate anything!"

"Does that mean all the branch directors will be doing all the paperwork you just taught me to do?"

"What do you think, Kathy? They are training someone on their staff the same as I did you. By the way, you caught onto it a whole lot quicker than some of the other branch assistants are."

"I would be happy to help out the other branches if they need it."

"Thanks Kathy, I'll be sure to let them know at the all-staff next week."

The following discussion between Scott Campbell and Jacob Jones takes place before the all-staff meeting held the next week.

"Scott, how are things out at Camp Tahoe and why are you here instead of out there processing paperwork?"

"Hello to you too, Jacob. I will have you know, I am able to be here because I have the greatest summer assistant in the world working for me. She is a whiz at this grant application processing thing. Yesterday, she processed over 20 applications, called and got the paperwork from another dozen or so, and was making calls to drum up more campers when I left this morning."

"That's great, Scott. I tried training an assistant to do this but I guess he is too young to get it. You would think a college senior would be able to understand a simple application process. He tried to process a few applications and ended up asking me a question every other minute. I finally gave up and took over the process myself. You wouldn't want to share Kathy with me would you?"

"Funny you should ask, Jacob because she mentioned the same thing to me last week. If she can get caught up with our applications this week, I'll send her out to you next Monday. You can only have her the one day but maybe it will be enough to get you started."

"Sounds like a plan, Scott."

Over the next month, Kathy Larson spends time at six branches helping with financial assistance applications.

During the fourth week of summer camp, Director Scott Campbell is talking with Kathy over toasted marshmallows.

"Hey Kathy, have I told you how wonderful all the other branch directors think you are? You have apparently saved the day for everyone but don't think this means you get a raise!"

"Oh, Scott, you know I would never leave this place. Where else can I sit and be eaten alive by mosquitoes while eating charred marshmallows? Besides, it has been fun getting out to see the other branches and helping outwith things. It makes me feel I am really making a difference."

"Something in your life seems to be making a difference, Kathy. Abby told me she saw you getting into a new car the other day at the mall. I guess things are not as tight this summer as you thought they would be."

"Oh, umm, Abby saw me at the mall? Was that last Thursday when I had my day off?"

"I'm not sure. It could have been. She only mentioned it in passing when I was in the Admin Offices Monday."

"Oh right, if it was last Thursday, that was the day I borrowed my neighbor's car as mine needed gas and I did not have any cash to fill it up. You know I can't afford a new car on what you pay me."

Two months later CFO, Abby Brooks, is working with Accounting Manager, Marcus Jenkins, to prepare the paperwork to close out the DHHS grant.

"Hmm, this is odd.. .1 wonder how it happened?"

"Abby, are you talking to yourself again? If you want to ask me a question, you will need to speak up!"

"Marcus, have you looked at these weekly branch reports? I did not have time to look over them earlier because the branches were handling all the reimbursement paperwork. Now that I have the time, I almost wish I hadn't looked at them."

"What do you mean Abby?"

"It's probably nothing but look at all these applications processed by 'KL.' The only employee who would have been involved in this with the initials of KL is Kathy Larson out at Camp Tahoe. If all these KLs are Kathy, why did she file for reimbursement on all these branch reports?"

"That's an easy one to answer, Abby. I heard one of the branch managers mention Kathy spent time at several of the branches this summer. Apparently, she was the only support type person who seemed to really understand how the grant application paperwork should be processed."

"Well, that explains it. I guess I'm too wired into potential fraud risks since my cousin started studying for her CFE exam. Every time we saw her over the summer, all I heard her talk about was fraud, being skeptical, and misappropriations."

"I guess when I saw Kathy in what looked to be a new car a few months ago, my fraud antennae went on the alert. Look here, Marcus. Do you see any pattern to any of these home addresses for the grant beneficiaries?"

"Hmm, let me see, Abby.. .It does look like we had a lot of participants coming from the 55512 and 55523 zip codes. Where are those by the way? They don't look familiar."

"Tell you what Marcus. If you will play fraud detective with me for an hour, I'll buy you lunch when we finish."

"Sounds good, Abby."

An hour later, Abby and Marcus are discussing the results of their research.

"Okay, Marcus, let's recap. According to our Internet searches we have no zip code 55523 but we do have a 55532. We do have a 55512 zip code but it doesn't look to be an area where families qualifying for financial assistance would live. Of the 10 names we checked, we found no record of seven of them. Because we used the Internet and phone book to search, I am not exactly sure what we can conclude from..."

Interrupting, Marcus says "Hang on a second, you have me thinking like a fraud detective now, and I'm thinking there might be a connection to this and Kathy Larsen. Where does she live?"

"Wait while I pull up the personnel system. What do you know? Kathy lives on Orange Avenue and the zip code is..."

"Don't tell me, it's either 55532 or 55512."

"You got it in two, Marcus. She is in 55512 which, if I remember correctly, is considered the low end of fashionable Park Centre. Maybe I should call my cousin and ask what her devious fraud mind makes of this. Like, what if she gave her friends and neighbors a reduced rate, dummied up a file for financial assistance, and then pocketed the reimbursement checks? What do you think, Marcus?"

"First, I think we need to do some more checking to figure out what may or may not be going on. Second I think we might want to run this with the auditors. They've been real hot on fraud the last few years. Third, I think you owe me lunch. We have earned at least lunch don't you think?"

EXERCISES

1. What elements of the fraud triangle[1] (that is, opportunity, incentive or pressure, and rationalization or attitude) are present in this case?

2. What additional procedures could the CFO have taken to detect this?

3. What, if any, internal controls are missing or inadequate that might indicate a potential for fraud exists in this case?

4. What types of preliminary audit procedures might detect this situation? What types of other audit procedures might detect this situation?

---

[1] Paragraph .A30 of AU-C section 240, *Consideration of Fraud in a Financial Statement Audit* (AICPA *Professional Standards*) (see course appendix A), states that three conditions are generally present when fraud occurs: opportunity, incentive or pressure, and rationalization or attitude. These three conditions are commonly referred to as the fraud triangle.

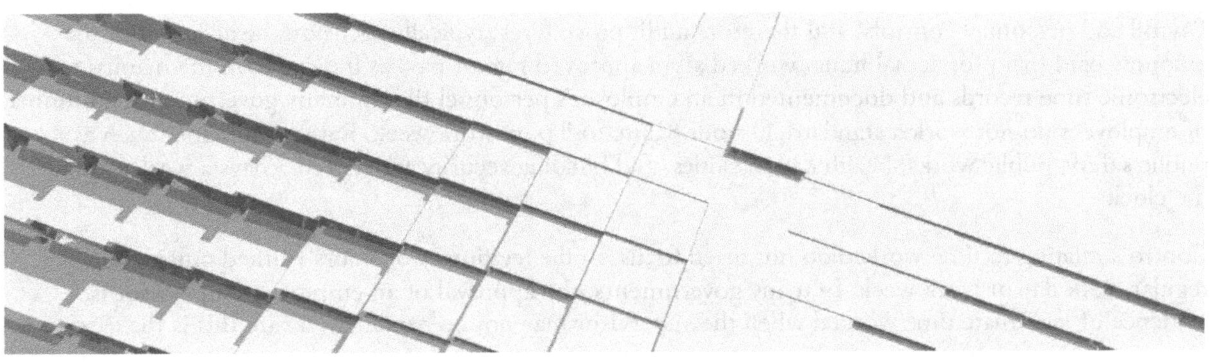

Chapter 3

Case 3: Personnel Fraud

Learning Objectives

After completing this chapter, you should be able to do the following:

- Determine how personnel policies and procedures in a fictitious government can be circumvented and lead to possible fraud or abuse.
- Determine the importance of identifying the environment in which a fictitious government entity operates and how it may affect the development and execution of personnel policies and procedures.

Before We Start

In many governmental organizations, salaries and benefits represent the major expenditure or expense category for most funds. Employees of governments are often paid less than their counterparts in the private sector which may lead some employees to rationalize misappropriation of assets as compensation for their low salary levels.

Indicators of personnel fraud include the following:

- Unusual or second-party endorsements on payroll check images
- Employees without the usual withholdings related to employer provided or offered benefits (that is, insurance, retirement, savings bonds, and the like)
- Missing, unusual looking, or altered time and attendance records in general or frequently for the same employee(s)
- Time and attendance records signed by someone other than the usual supervisor in general or frequently for the same employee(s)

Payroll and personnel controls, and therefore audit procedures, typically focus on the accuracy of the amounts paid (paid for actual hours worked at an approved rate of pay) as indicated on the manual or electronic time records and documented in an employee's personnel file. In many governments, a number of employees do not work a standard 40-hour 8 a.m. to 5 p.m. work week. Rather, functions such as public safety, public works, health care facilities, and building security are staffed 7 days a week around the clock.

Controls relating to time worked do not often focus on the legitimacy of hours worked outside the regular work day or work week. In many governments, the approval of an employee's supervisor is evidence of legitimate time worked when the supervisor may not be personally aware this is the case.

THE CASE

The following conversation takes place between three public safety employees of the town of Sea Side during shift change.

"Hey, Billy, what is this I heard about you getting married?"

"That's right, Jim, I bit a bullet last Saturday night and asked Jessie to marry me. Much to my surprise she said 'yes' so here I am an engaged man. I think she and her mother have us getting married month after next."

Jim looks around the locker room and says "Greg, did you hear Billy's news? He has gone and got himself engaged. Sounds like he is already being told what to do, what do you think?"

"Well, I think if he wants to start this marriage off right, he should do what I did and take a two-week cruise for a honeymoon. My wife still gets all misty-eyed when she looks at the pictures and that was over five years ago. What do you think of a cruise, Billy?"

"It sounds like a great idea Greg, but I think a weekend at the beach might be all we can afford. I am only a low-paid, second-year patrolman and you are a highly paid training officer. Come to think of it, how were you able to afford a two-week cruise for your honeymoon? You had only been on the force a year or two at that time."

"What do you say, Jim? Do we let this not-much-better-than-a-rookie in on the secret to a financially secure future?"

"Sure Greg. It's like this Billy, once you have proven yourself, you become part of the team and we all take care of each other. Last year when Suzie was buying her house and needed help with the down payment a couple of us remember being trained by her Daddy and saw fit to help her outwith things."

"What do you mean, Jim? Suzie earned that down payment by working eight straight weekends of overtime. I don't mean any disrespect, but I don't see you helped her with that at all."

"How do you think she got to work all of that overtime? Didn't it seem odd to you that Suzie was the one always being called in when someone was sick or taking a vacation day?"

"But, but, Greg, Jim, I really don't get what you are saying here."

"Okay, Jim, I'll try to explain it this time. Look, Billy, when one of us needs a little financial help, the rest of us work to make things happen. Someone will ask you to cover for them the next time they want a day off and you say 'sure.' Other times, you're the one up next on the overtime list, and one of us knows you need some help, so we call in sick. Most of us make half our salary in overtime every year. Why do you think our lieutenants fight so hard to stay in the bargaining unit?"

"I guess I never thought much about it. What do I have to do to get some extra hours the next few months to pay for a honeymoon? I don't know if I have the time or energy to work enough overtime for a two-week cruise but I could try."

"Billy, you just leave things to me andjim and the rest of us. We will take care of you. After all, you're one of us now."

KNOWLEDGE CHECK

1. Which of the following is accurate of the town of Sea Side?

   a. The police department does not allow employees to work overtime.
   b. Billy does not have any pressure on him to earn enough to take his future wife on a nice honeymoon.
   c. There appears to be either fraud or abuse occurring with respect to overtime in the police department.
   d. Sea Side contracts with the county to provide law enforcement services to town residents.

A few months later, the town of Sea Side hired a new town manager, Larry Patton.

Prior to joining the town of Sea Side, Larry was the finance director for a medium-sized city. The town council hired Larry for his financial expertise and economic development experience. One of the first things Larry did when he accepted the job was to ask for a copy of the town's audited financial statements for the past three years, a copy of the budget for the last three years, and current year-to-date budget reports.

Soon after starting his new job with the town of Sea Side, Larry met with the finance director, Lynette Odom.

"Come on in Lynette. I have been looking forward to our meeting since we scheduled it a few weeks ago. I hate to say it, but the good news and the bad news is your new boss is a bean counter. Please let me know if I try to micro-manage things with you, okay?"

"Well, uh, sure, Larry. I am actually looking forward to having someone in charge who knows something about accounting and finance. We are a small shop here and getting good controls and procedures in place has been a little tough. Like most finance officials in small towns, I have to wear all kinds of hats."

"Believe me. I understand where you are coming from. I may not have ever worked in a small city finance department, but I still remember wearing the HR and IT hats when I first went to work at my last job! How many hats are you wearing today?"

Laughing, "Well today I am wearing my Budget Czar hat which means our meeting could not be at a better time. I want to answer any questions you might have; then, if we still have time I would like to talk to you about some of my concerns."

"That sounds fine with me Lynette. First, I am pleased to see that you prepared a CAFR the last two years even though you are the only professional on staff and probably worked weekends to get it completed on time. It is a real indication of quality and professionalism as far as I am concerned. Second, from the last three annual financial statements, I noticed there are significant differences between original and final budget amounts for several functions. From your discussion in the MD&A the last two years, it looks like you have had significant overtime in the public safety and public works functions. Is that from some sort of staff shortage, or what? Looking at the budgets, I did not notice any huge differences in budgeted and actual FTEs."

"Believe it or not Larry, this is one of the things I want to talk to you about. Let's save this part of our discussion until you have asked all of your questions."

Larry agrees and he and Lynette spend the next half hour going over the budgets, financial statements, and the projections for the current year. Rocking back in his chair, Larry listens to Lynette's issues.

"One of the things going on here is probably no different than what goes on in hundreds of towns and cities across the United States. Unfortunately, I was born and raised in Sea Side and I hate seeing this town spend money unwisely. I can't prove anything, Larry, but I think our police, fire, and public works personnel are ripping off the town."

"What do you mean Lynette?"

"I have analyzed the annual earnings of all our employees for the last three years. Here, look at this spreadsheet where I indicate the base pay, gross pay, function, and position for each employee. I highlighted those employees whose W-2 gross earnings are 150 percent or more of their base pay. You can see the functional summary at the bottom."

"Hmm, this is interesting. It looks like a lot of the town's employees earned well over their base pay. It also looks as though a lot of them made more money than their department head! Is this right, did almost all fire and police personnel in the bargaining unit earn 50 percent of their base pay in overtime? What prompted you to do this in-depth analysis, anyway?"

"Actually, I have to give my payroll clerk, Richard, credit for this. I have only been the finance director the last 18 months and before that I worked part time for a large CPA firm while I finished my master's degree and studied for the CPA exam. Before the town council hired me, the town clerk acted as the finance officer. The town clerk meant well, but she is not a degreed accountant and did not like to cross the other department heads. You will learn, Larry, this is a very small town."

"Okay, back to your question. Richard asked me for a raise when I first got here and when I asked why, he said it was because he was one of the lowest paid employees in the town. I thought he might be mistaken and asked him to pull together some salary information for me. What he gave me was the W-2 reconciliation printout for the current year. When I looked at it I could not believe how well paid the employees were and I began to think I needed a raise as well as Richard. He pointed out to me the W-2 wages included overtime and for many employees there was a large difference in their base pay and their gross annual wages. Together we pulled the information on all the employees that I used to prepare this schedule."

"So, Lynette, what is it you think is going on here?"

"I am not sure about the fire and police personnel, but I have it on good authority the public works employees are logging overtime on weekends and not necessarily working. Also, it seems everyone gets called out at least twice during the week they are on call. We have a two-hour call out pay minimum for our public works employees when they are the designated 'on call' employee. My hands are tied because as long as the time cards are signed by the employees and their supervisor, I have to pay them the hours on the card."

"Do you have any suspicions about the overtime in the fire and police departments?"

"I only have my suspicions and, as long as you remember they are only suspicions, I will let you know what I think. Last year, during the budget process, I suggested to the police and fire chiefs they ask for additional personnel because their overtime budget requests were so large. Did you notice that last year the fire department had overtime equal to 50 percent of its salary expenditures and the police department had overtime equal to 35 percent of its budgeted salaries? Well, I did, and using the base salaries of entry level patrol officers and EMTs and their initial equipment needs I figured we could hire six additional EMTs and nine additional patrol officers. When I suggested this to each of the chiefs they basically patted me on the head and told me to go home and bake some brownies."

Arching an eyebrow Larry said, "Brownies?"

"Well, they didn't actually say to bake brownies but it is what their patronizing attitudes said. They both gave me some techno-speak about minimum manning levels and shift change differentials. I knew they were trying to snow me and I had a budget to balance so I let it go. I still wondered, though, why they wouldn't even discuss the idea of hiring additional personnel in order to decrease their overtime budgets."

Knowledge Check

2. Which describes the town of Sea Side?

    a. Few of the town's employees earn well over their base pay.
    b. One of the first things the new town manager requested was a copy of the budget for the last five years.
    c. When factoring in overtime a lot of the town employees make more money than their department heads.
    d. All of the town's employees are exempt from federal requirements to pay overtime for hours worked in excess of 40 hours per week.

3. Which is accurate of the town of Sea Side?

    a. The town of Sea Side is a large metropolitan beach-front community.
    b. The finance director describes the town as a small shop where getting good controls and procedures in place has been a little tough.
    c. The finance director is not looking forward to working for the new town manager who knows something about accounting and finance.
    d. The finance director is not happy in her job.

"Not to worry, Lynette. This year it will be me asking the questions when they submit their budget requests. Can you get me the paperwork you did last year calculating the number of personnel we could afford in lieu of overtime?"

"Also, Lynette, have you talked to our auditors about this? I know where I came from our auditors talked to employees all over the city about where they thought fraud might be occurring or if they thought they worked with honest people. What did our auditors do here the last few years with respect to fraud?"

"I will tell you this Larry, if I had not studied the auditor's responsibilities with respect to fraud for the CPA exam I would not know it existed based on our town auditors. You will probably learn soon enough that we only have two CPA firms in town and one has been here forever and one has been here five years. Bet you can't guess which one does the audit?"

"I'm thinking it's not the new kid on the block. Please don't tell me the audit partner is related to someone on the town council."

"No such luck, Larry. Sorry, but our Mayor's uncle's wife's brother-in-law is the partner on our audit. I don't think the firm has any other audit clients except for the town and the local bank. I ran a license check on the principals last year using the State Board of Accountancy database and they all still had licenses. Not to be ugly or anything, but I wouldn't be surprised if they earn all their CPE at those free web-based sessions several of the national firms offer. If not that, they probably go to an 8-hour class and sit in the back of the room checking their email, Facebook, and Twitter accounts and reading e-books instead of listening to the discussion leader!"

"That's enough Lynette. You have given me a lot to think about and I appreciate your candor. I don't think I need to ask you to keep this conversation between the two of us, do I?"

"No, Larry. Let me know if you need any additional information."

KNOWLEDGE CHECK

4. Which is accurate of the town of Sea Side?

    a. Prior to joining the town of Sea Side, the town manager worked for a small city.
    b. The town council hired the new town manager for his financial expertise and economic development experience.
    c. The finance director recently received his CGMA certification.
    d. The town manager is a practicing CPA.

Upon returning to his office, Larry looks over the collective bargaining agreements between the town and its police, fire, and public works personnel. He also reads up on the payroll procedures. Based on this review, he ascertains there are no controls assuring overtime has been paid for actual work other than the signature of a supervisor on a time card. Looking over the management letters from prior years, he notes there have been no comments made by the auditors regarding payroll procedures or any other control deficiencies. Finding this a little strange, he calls the audit firm to schedule a meeting with the engagement partner.

EXERCISES

1. Are there any potential fraud risks in this case? If so, what are they?

2. What helpful procedures could the auditor have performed in prior years with respect to the issues raised in this case?

3. What additional controls should be in place with respect to payroll processing?

4. What would be your recommendations to the new town manager if you were the audit partner on this engagement?

5. Would any of the situations described in this case be considered fraud or abuse?

Chapter 4

Case 4: Grant Expense Allocations

Learning Objectives

After completing this chapter, you should be able to do the following:

- Analyze how procurement and expense allocation policies in a fictitious not-for-profit (NFP) entity can be circumvented and lead to possible fraud.
- Identify types of audit procedures typically effective in responding to the fraud risks discussed in this case.

Before We Start

Grantors and grant recipients may have a long-term and close relationship which could create fraud risks. For example, an NFP may be the only organization in a rural area that is able to provide certain services to a targeted population. Likewise, an NFP may have an excellent reputation in the community or region relating to the provision of specific types of services. In these situations, a grantor might be willing to provide less oversight to such organizations in exchange for the NFP providing exclusive or high quality services (or both) to program beneficiaries. Therefore, the auditor will need to determine what relationships exist between their NFP clients and the granting agencies and their personnel.

An inherent fraud risk in NFPs receiving grants is that they may feel pressure to misstate functional amounts to comply with grant provisions or debt covenants. Additionally, mission-driven employees and directors may be willing to allocate unallowable costs to grants in order to provide more program services.

THE CASE

Seniors Forever is a 501(c)(3) corporation whose mission is to enrich the lives of senior citizens in six counties. Most of its funding comes from state grants with a minor amount of funding coming from contributions and charges for services.

Kevin Morgan, the district program director for Seniors Forever is having lunch with a college friend and former colleague, Joann Ford, who is a local case manager with the state Department of Human Services.

"Joann, I cannot believe it has been six months since we were last able to get together for lunch. How are the twins and your husband doing?"

"All three of them keep me running 24/7 and some mornings I think I have two-year old triplets instead of two-year old twins! How are you and your wife handling being new parents?"

"It's great, especially for me because I only have diaper duty on the weekends. Here's our server, ready to order?"

"Good idea."

After their orders are taken Joann and Kevin catch up on what is going on in their professional lives and with their employers. Over lunch they have the following conversation.

"Hey, Joann, what is going on in the Capitol these days with the new governor preparing her first budget?"

"Well, I'm not as connected as I used to be but rumor has it she is out to make a very loud policy statement with this first budget. My boss told me he heard there were going to be major cuts in social programs in order to fund the new class size statute and the law enforcement referendum from last election."

"Is there any word on the specific programs that are targeted for cuts? Does Seniors Forever have anything to worry about?"

"As of yet, my boss has not heard anything specific. Our office speculates it would be difficult for the governor to propose major cuts in education and indigent health care because those were the cornerstones of her campaign last fall. Our people on the Hill think she would get a lot of pushback from the legislature if she tried to take too much away from seniors, though. After all, this state is the retirement capital of the world."

"At least that is encouraging news. Could you keep me posted on anything else you hear?"

"Sure thing, Kevin."

A week later, Kevin gets a call from Joann.

"Hey there, Joann. What is going on?"

"Kevin, the governor released her executive budget late yesterday and all kinds of chaos is breaking loose today. Turn on the television if you can to catch what they are saying about it on the Hill and call me back."

"Joann, I work for a not-for-profit and don't exactly have a television in my office. The CEO is the only person with one of those in their office. Tell me what is going on."

"You will still need to catch some more details but here is the bottom line affecting you and me."

"The governor is proposing a massive state-wide agency reorganization. Basically, any agency not mandated by the Constitution or statute is being overhauled, eliminated, or consolidated with other agencies. Her proposal has Human Services, Citizens First, and Sunshine Health combining into one agency with most of the services being contracted rather than performed by state employees. She also proposes that all existing contracts with auto-renewal provisions not be renewed unless the contractors are showing significant progress in improving the quality of life for their program recipients."

"Wow, that is huge for your department as well as my folks here at Seniors. We have some very large existing contracts with those agencies that we had expected would be automatically renewed. In fact, we bought two vans to expand our transportation services in two counties believing the existing contracts would be extended."

"That is really unfortunate for Seniors, Kevin. I would suggest you make those programs look as good as they can for the remaining months you have the contracts. If the decision makers see you are making a real difference, they might be amenable to executing the auto-renewal options."

"I appreciate the heads up, Joann, but forgive me if I'm not too happy about it."

"If there is anything I can do for you, let me know."

The next day Kevin schedules a meeting with the program directors and managers to update them on the situation.

"So this is it, people. We have got to make these programs look like they are changing lives or we may not have jobs next funding cycle. I had our accounting manager join us today to summarize where we are with these programs. Ned, the floor is all yours."

"Thanks Kevin. I didn't want to bore all of you with bean counter talk so I prepared this summary of the existing state-funded programs we have. The biggest program is the Nutrition First program which allows us to provide hot meals to all our seniors five days a week. This is a five-year program and we are in the last year. During this last contract cycle, the state gave us $2,000,000 each year and we are able to charge administrative and overhead costs to this program."

"Our second biggest program is in the second year of a five-year contract and gives us $500,000 each year to subsidize adult day care for seniors in Tangerine County. We use most of this money to offset the cost of the day care program we offer here at the district office."

"As you can see from the schedule, the Keep on Truckin' program is funded primarily with three state grants. The first grant is a three-year 'maintenance grant' that provides us $100,000 each year for maintenance of our van fleet. This is supposed to cover our gasoline as well routine maintenance expenses. Most years we have not used all the funds because we did not operate that many vehicles. I expect that will change this year because we bought the two new vans last year and because gas prices have been erratic this past year. We have one more year left on this grant."

"The second 'transportation grant' provides us $100,000 annually to subsidize transportation for seniors in Water and Geronimo counties. We also received an additional $60,000 for this program last year, which bought the two new vans we are using now. We are in the third year of a five-year contract."

"Our last grant in the Keep on Truckin' program is a three-year 'bus grant' which gives us $50,000 annually to subsidize bus passes for seniors in Tangerine County. We have two more years on this contract."

"Thanks Ned. This summary you prepared is great. What do you mean with this footnote about 'cost allocations'?"

"Well Kevin, some of our grants reimburse us for shared costs. For example, I allocate the costs of the salaries of the staff in our Water and Geronimo county offices to the 'transportation grant' and the accounting department costs to all our grants. Most of the time, we have more costs to allocate than we are allowed reimbursement for under the grants."

"What do you mean, Ned?"

"Most taxpayers, and grantors, want to see grant monies spent on program beneficiaries rather than subsidizing overhead costs. Many federal and state grants do not allow much, if any, recovery of administrative costs. I guess the rationale is if grant-funded programs have enough funding for overhead, then they short-changed the funding for beneficiaries. We would probably look better to the Legislature if we funded all of our administrative costs with non-grant funds. I would love to do this but we simply do not have the financial resources to be that generous, Kevin."

"Thanks a lot, Ned. You gave us a lot to think about and I appreciate it."

KNOWLEDGE CHECK

1. Which is accurate of Seniors Forever?

   a. The governor is proposing a massive state-wide agency reorganization that could affect Seniors Forever.
   b. The smallest state-funded program is the Nutrition First program which allows Seniors Forever to provide hot meals to seniors five days a week.
   c. The largest state-funded program is Keep on Truckin'.
   d. Most of the funding for Seniors Forever comes from federal grants.

After Ned leaves the room, Kevin looks at his program directors and managers and tells them what he was thinking during Ned's presentation.

"Listen up ladies and gentlemen. I think I have a way to make us look as good as we can in the next state funding cycle. I don't know how many of you were following what Ned was saying about that administrative recovery thing or not, but I sure was. Starting today, we are going to charge as many direct program costs to these state-funded programs as we can. We are not going to leave any money for Ned to use for administrative costs… What's the problem, Josh?"

"I know I am stuck out in the wilds of Water County but I'm not sure how I can do this. As far as I know, we will not have enough direct costs because administrative cost recovery was part of our proposal for the 'transportation grant'."

"Kevin, not to rain on your parade or anything but as the manager of the Nutrition First program I know it was designed to help offset some of the costs of running the district office. It seems as if we would be biting off our nose to spite our face if you want to only charge direct costs to these programs."

"Well, Ana aren't you the queen of trite expressions this morning! If all of you are having problems with this, then you can start sending all of your purchase orders and check requests to me for approval and I will make sure we get things charged to these grants that will help us keep the programs going!"

"That is not what I meant, Kevin. I'll be a team player, just tell me what you want me to do."

"Thanks for your support, Ana. I am going to assume she speaks for the rest of you as well. I want all of you to monitor all your costs each week. Before the end of the month, if it looks as if you are going to have money left, buy supplies in advance or charge expenses from some other program to these state grant programs. We must have half a dozen programs using food and paper products, Ana. Charge those to Nutrition First if you need to. Josh, the district officers will help with that extra gas thing by charging the gas in our corporate cars to the 'maintenance grant'. If we need to, we can use 'bus grant' funds to buy passes for our employees. Do all of you get the idea now?"

Grumbling, all those present agree to Kevin's ideas and leave for their respective offices. As they are leaving Ana turns to Josh.

"Josh, I know Kevin's heart is in the right place, but do you know if what he wants us to do is illegal? Working for a not-for-profit all these years has not always provided me job security but at least I have always known I would not be in jail."

"Don't worry, Ana. I think Kevin has the right idea. This organization would have to close its doors if we lost these grants. Where would all of our seniors be then?"

Over the next several months, charges are made against the grants as had been discussed in the meeting with Kevin. At the end of the grant period, there are no funds remaining for recovery of administrative costs and the programs look very successful to the legislature. All of the programs are automatically renewed.

KNOWLEDGE CHECK

2. Which is accurate of Seniors Forever?

    a. The Keep on Truckin' program is funded primarily by user fees.
    b. The second biggest state-funded program is in the second of a five-year contract and gives Seniors Forever $500,000 each year to subsidize adult day care for seniors in Tangerine County.
    c. Seniors Forever has only one grant to fund all of its programs.
    d. One grant funding the Keep on Truckin' program is a four-year "bus grant" that provides $90,000 annually to subsidize bus passes for seniors in Tangerine County.

EXERCISES

1. Do any of the situations described in this case study represent fraud? If so, what situations and what type of fraud?

2. What types of preliminary audit procedures might have detected this situation?

3. What types of other audit procedures might have detected this situation?

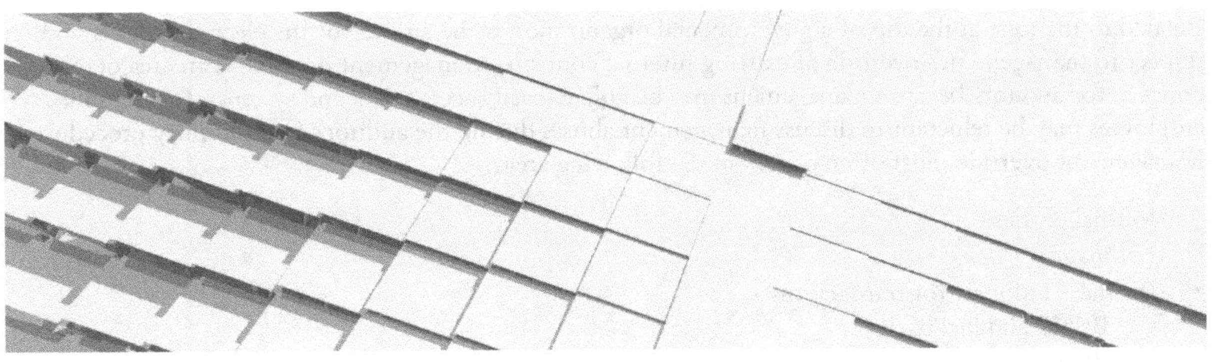

Chapter 5

Case 5: Management Override

Learning Objectives

After completing this chapter, you should be able to do the following:

- Identify how the governing board of a fictitious government can put pressure on staff to complete projects.
- Identify how management override of internal controls can lead to possible fraud in a fictitious government.

Before We Start

The political process varies by type, size, and nature of government, but in all cases the process places constant pressure on elected officials and other policymakers. In turn, elected officials and policy makers may put pressure on management and employees to achieve program results, provide more and higher quality services with fewer resources, or to provide resources for projects that are important to them personally.

If the "tone at the top" of a governmental organization is one of zero tolerance and fraudsters are promptly disciplined, employees may be less likely to commit fraud. A positive and open work environment, at all levels of the organization, also helps in preventing, detecting, and deterring fraud. Therefore, it is important for the auditor of governmental organizations to obtain a thorough understand of a government's control environment when performing risk assessment procedures.

Related to the tone at the top of a governmental organization is the attitude of the elected officials with respect to management's override of existing internal controls. Management override is an area of concern for auditors because management may be able to easily access data and systems. In addition, employees may be reluctant to discuss management abuses during the auditor's fraud inquiry procedures. Management override most often occurs in the following areas:

- Journal entries
- Estimates
- Business rationale for transactions
  - Bribes and kickbacks
  - Billing schemes

THE CASE

The following exchange occurs during the first budget hearing for the city of Pleasantville (held in late August which is approximately five weeks prior to the end of the fiscal year). In addition to the commission members, staff members present include Sam Meyer, city manager; Ava Bacall, finance director; Lauren Gardner, budget director; Judy Monroe, city clerk; and other department directors.

"Commissioner Bogart you may have the floor."

"Thank you Mayor Humphries. I noticed in reviewing next year's budget we included $25,000 for a citizen survey. Correct me if I'm wrong, but I thought we wanted to survey our citizens early this fall to be consistent with the survey we had done three years ago. If this is the case, why was the money not budgeted for this year?"

"Mr. City Manager, would you care to address Commissioner Bogart's question?"

"Mayor Humphries, Commissioner Bogart. Your recollection is correct in that the council wished to conduct the survey in the early fall as was done three years ago. The funds for the consultant to conduct the survey were budgeted for this year. Unfortunately, other projects took priority both in time and money causing me to include the funds in my next year's..."

Commissioner Bergman interrupts saying "Wait just a minute there. What do you mean other projects took priority and money? As you may or may not recall, the citizen survey was my idea years ago and I do not appreciate you not making it a priority this year especially because you had the money in your budget!"

"Hold on there, Commissioner Bergman, we will show courtesy and respect for any meeting I am chairing!"

"I apologize, Mayor, if you felt I was being discourteous or disrespectful. It just gets my goat that our city manager could have forgotten something as important as our tri-annual citizen survey. Is there any way we can get it going before the end of the year?"

"Mr. City Manager, what do you think? Is it possible to get the survey going sooner rather than later?"

"Well, Mr. Mayor, this is a very busy time for the staff what with the public hearings on the budget and getting ready for year end. Besides, there is the issue of funding..."

Commissioner Bogart interrupts saying "Mr. City Manager, I am extremely tired of you singing the 'we do not have any money' song every time we ask you if something can be done that you did not think of! What happened to the money we budgeted for the survey, anyway? The way I see it, you and your staff forgot about this survey so you can remember it now. What do you have to say for yourself?"

"Mr. Mayor, Commissioners. Please let's not get worked up over nothing. As you may recall, the annual volunteer recognition banquet last spring cost more than I had budgeted. Knowing at that time we would not be able to conduct the citizen survey this year, I used the money budgeted for the survey to cover the additional cost of the volunteer banquet. However, I am sure our budget director, Ms. Gardner, can find the money for the survey somewhere in what is left of this year's budget. Ms. Gardner, what are your thoughts on this?"

"Well, um, I think, um, well, there is always the contingency fund. Last time I checked, I think there was like $50,000 left in it. With formal approval by the commission tonight, we could maybe, um, start the procurement process like, um, probably sometime next week, I think."

"Mayor, I move we approve $25,000 from the commission contingency fund be used for a citizen survey."

"Thank you Commissioner Bergman. Do I hear a second?"

"Second."

"I have a motion and a second, any discussion? Hearing none, all in favor signify by saying 'aye'. AH opposed?"

"Motion passes. Mr. City Manager, get working on the citizen survey and do us all a favor and make it a 'priority' will you? I don't know about the rest of the commission, but I am getting a little tired of your excuses. Do you understand what I'm saying?"

"Yes, Mayor. The staff and I will get right on this tomorrow."

Later that week, finance director A va Bacall, runs into Sam Meyer, the city manager, and Judy Monroe, the city clerk, getting coffee.

"Sam, the commission was a little rough on you at the meeting this week. Is there anything I can do to help with the survey process? It is getting close to year end but my staff and I are in pretty good shape and could spare some time to get some quotes or do some research for you."

"Thanks for the offer, Ava, but I have Lauren and her budget staff working on this project. She and her staff were fairly instrumental in assisting the consultant with the last survey."

"Well, if they need any help, let me know. At this time of year, I know Lauren and her staff are busy fielding budget questions from citizens and might not have time to get quotes or research qualifications of consultants."

"Will do, Ava."

KNOWLEDGE CHECK

1. Which is accurate of the city of Pleasantville?

    a. Commission members approved $25,000 from the commission contingency fund be used for a citizen survey.
    b. Commission members told the city manager to delay the citizen survey.
    c. The city does not utilize a contingency fund.
    d. Two commission members did not approve funding the citizen survey from the contingency fund.

About two weeks later, Ava is reviewing and approving purchase orders and runs across a purchase order for consulting services related to the citizen survey in the amount of $25,000.

She looks at the attached documentation and finds only the portion of the minutes of the commission meeting approving the funding of the survey from their contingency fund. Upon further review, Ava notes the purchase order was originated by budget director Lauren Gardner and approved by Sam Meyer, the city manager.

Because the city's purchasing policy requires formal bids for any consulting-related services single purchase of $25,000 or more, she heads off to Lauren's office to find out what is going on with the survey.

"Hey Lauren, do you have a few minutes for a question or two?"

"Oh Ava, I am in the middle of something right now, can it wait?"

"This won't take long, I promise. It's about the purchase order for the consultant doing the citizen survey..."

"Well, I don't know what your problem is with it because it was clearly approved by the commission. I even attached that portion of the minutes to the purchase order as documentation."

"The problem is even though the commission approved the funding, they did not specifically approve this vendor nor did they authorize you violating our purchasing policy. I know things have been hectic for you, but surely you remembered that we have to go through the bid process for consulting services of $25,000 or more?"

"I did not forget; I simply did not think it was necessary because the commission approved it. I will call the consultant and see if he is willing to take $24,900. He did our last survey three years ago and $100 should not be a deal breaker for him. Will that make you happy, Ava?"

"Lauren, I don't really think that is working within the spirit of our purchasing policy. If you can get the consultant to agree to the $24,900 and as long as you get quotes from at least two other bona fide consultants that are not less than his, I guess I can approve it."

"What do you mean I have to get quotes? He did our survey the last time and that makes him a sole source provider."

"Lauren, the fact that he did our survey the last time does not make him a sole source provider. In this day and age, citizen surveys are not rocket science and there are a lot of qualified and affordable consultants out there doing them."

"Okay, Okay. I will get the quotes."

After leaving Lauren's office, Ava stops by the office of Jimmy Grant, accounts payable supervisor, to bring him up to speed on the situation and ask him to bring the corrected paperwork to her as soon as it is received.

A week later, Jimmy Grant brings Ava the paper work for the survey consultant, as resubmitted by the budget director, Lauren Gardner.

"Ava, I thought you would want to see this. By the way, do not shoot the messenger."

"What do you mean...I cannot believe she did this! Not only did she not get any quotes for but she authorized the consultant to start work! Look at this, Jimmy, she even attached the first invoice for payment. The nerve of her, doesn't she remember anything about the reason for our purchasing controls?"

"Now Ava, calm down. Do you want me to go and ask her where the quotes are and why the consultant was allowed to start work before the purchase order was approved?"

"Would you? At this point I don't think I could keep my temper."

Knowledge Check

2. Which is accurate of the city of Pleasantville?

   a. A $25,000 purchase order for a citizen survey was originated by the budget director and approved by the city manager.
   b. A $24,900 purchase order for a citizen survey was originated by the budget director and approved by the city manager.
   c. Formal bids were received on the citizen survey in accordance with the city's purchasing policy.
   d. The city undergoes an annual citizen survey.

A few minutes later, Jimmy returns to Ava's office shaking his head.

"You are not going to believe this. She said she did not have to get quotes because Sam agreed with her the consultant was a sole source vendor. You are going to love this next part. She said she authorized the work before approval because Sam signed the purchase order. According to her, if the city manager signs a purchase order, it should not need your approval before it can be executed."

Banging her head against her desk, Ava says "This has to be one of the stupidest turf wars I have ever seen. At least she could have remembered to attach a sole source justification to all this paperwork. Give me all of the paperwork and I'll get her to at least prepare a memo. Rest assured, I am not signing the purchase order nor will I sign off on the sole source justification. Do me a favor and write me a short memo to document your conversation with Lauren today."

"No problem, I'll get it to you by 5:00 today."

"Thanks Jimmy, and I'm sorry to have dragged you into this. I will write my version of events as well and then attach them as additional documentation for this monumental mistake."

EXERCISES

1. Does this case present a type of fraud risk? If so, what type of fraud risk?

2. Which part, if any, of the fraud triangle is represented in this case? Explain your response.

3. What type of preliminary audit procedures might detect this type of situation?

4. If preliminary audit procedures did not detect this type of situation, what type of other audit procedures could be performed that might detect this situation?

5. How would you have handled this situation if you were the finance director?

Chapter 6

Case 6: Pledges and Contributions

Learning Objectives

After completing this chapter, you should be able to do the following:

- Determine how various board incentives and mandates in a fictitious not-for-profit (NFP) entity may be possible indicators of fraud.
- Identify how the fraud triangle may affect audit planning in an audit of a fictitious NFP involved in major fundraising.

Before We Start

An inherent fraud risk in NFPs is the incentive to overstate revenues or results in an effort to obtain additional grant funds or contributions from resource providers. Although pledge receivables are not technically "accounts" receivable from a legal and accounting perspective, the indicators of receivable fraud are appropriate "proxies" for indicators of fraud in pledges receivables.

Indicators of receivable fraud include the following:

- Unexplained differences noted on receivable confirmations received
- Significant or unusual adjustments to receivable records
- Amounts deposited inconsistent with amounts due
- Significant credit balances in receivable accounts

Another fraud risk inherent in many NFPs receiving contributions is that NFPs may feel pressure to misstate functional amounts to maximize program expenses. Additionally, mission-driven employees and directors may be willing to misrepresent amounts in the financial statements in order to provide more program services.

THE CASE

We Care is a 501(c)(3) whose mission is to provide temporary assistance to female victims of domestic violence and their dependent children. In addition to operating a temporary living facility, We Care provides technical training to women residents and child care for their pre-school aged children. The We Care shelter was constructed with an anonymous bequest 20 years ago and is in need of remodeling and expansion.

We Care has a strong reputation in the local community and funds its operations with a number of grants and a strong annual fundraising campaign. At a recent meeting, the board of directors approved plans to expand the existing shelter to house an additional 20 residents and to construct a new shelter in the southern portion of the county. The estimated cost to expand the existing facility is $2,500,000 and the projected cost to permit and build the new facility is $5,500,000.

To fund construction, the Board authorized the CEO, Jan Damon, to solicit proposals from area banks for construction and permanent financing. After visiting a number of area banks, Jan has learned the banks will not offer We Care financing because no steady revenue stream exists to secure payment. However, two banks indicated that with We Care's proven track record of its annual fundraising campaign, it should be easy to raise the needed funds with a capital campaign.

At an executive committee meeting, Jan brings up the possibility of bank financing for the proposed construction projects. Present at the meeting are Toni Grant, President; Susan Ross, Vice President; Tom Mayer, Treasurer; and Jan Damon.

"Toni, based on my conversations with several area banks, we will not be able to obtain financing for the expansion or new shelter unless we have a secure revenue source for repayment. Two loan officers suggested we have a capital campaign to raise the needed funds."

"Jan, we know how successful we have been in raising funds for our annual appeal. What do the rest of you think about a capital campaign for these two new projects?"

"Toni, as treasurer, I think it would be worth trying to raise the funds. Worst case, we don't raise anything, best case, we raise more than we need."

Laughing, Susan Ross says "Tom, you are always such an optimist! I don't have any problem with the idea but I am concerned about whether or not we have the people, time, and expertise to take on this large of a fundraising effort. Jan, what do you think?"

"Well, our current development director, Mike Moran, had experience at his last job with a capital campaign. I don't recall how successful he was but I know I have heard him talking about it. I will research what this type of a campaign would take and talk to Mike about it. I will get back with you before our next Board meeting."

During the next week, Jan and Mike contact a colleague of theirs, Sam Rogers, at the Community Foundation to ask about the challenges associated with their recent capital campaign.

"Well, six years ago we were successful primarily because we took the time to plan our campaign strategy. Making a case for capital dollars is a lot different than making a case for operating funds. You need..."

Interrupting, Mike says "Sam, I realize the approach is different and I'm wondering what you did specifically in the planning stage to make your campaign successful."

"We used a fundraising consultant to help us develop our strategy, identify potential donors, and work out our timing. I think what made us successful was the training we gave our volunteers and our rigid adherence to the time line. Our board felt we had a very narrow window of time for our case to be relevant which meant we had only 12 months to meet our goal. We were also very fortunate to receive several large pledges early in the campaign from some of our community leaders."

"Our board definitely has a compelling case. Because they feel so strongly about this need in the community, they would want any capital campaign to be completed as soon as possible. Do you think it could be done in less than 12 months?"

"I don't know, Jan. A lot would depend on your leadership and your volunteers. It could happen. You are looking to raise less than half of what we were and your base of support is almost as broad as ours. Do you want me to send you copies of what we did for our campaign?"

"That would be great, Sam, and thanks."

Leaving, Mike and Jan discuss what they learned from Sam.

"Look Jan, I know we can do this. I had some good experience when I worked as the assistant development director at Healthy Families. What if I take Sam's information and develop a proposal for you to review and then take to the board?"

"Okay, Mike, go for it."

The next week Jan reviews the capital campaign plan prepared by Mike. After asking a few questions and having Mike make a few changes, Jan presents it to the executive committee. Having no comments or suggestions, the executive committee places the capital campaign on the agenda for the next board meeting where it is approved unanimously.

The day after the board meeting, Jan calls together her senior staff including Mike Moran.

"I guess all of you have heard the news that we are going to embark on a capital campaign to see if we can raise funds for our expansion project and new facility. This is going to take all of us working closely with the board and other community volunteers if we want to succeed. We have a time line of 12 months to get the money raised and Mike has a great plan to get us there. Mike, will you go over everything with the group?"

Mike spends the next 10 minutes outlining the strategy and responsibilities associated with the capital campaign. At the end, the only question is from the facility director, Amy Green.

"Mike, my only question is who will be doing our regular jobs while we are all out asking for money? I barely have enough time in my day as it is right now. How am I supposed to protect abused women, educate their children, and raise money all in a 24-hour day?"

"I realize it sounds like a lot, Amy, but I really don't think it will be that much additional work for you. You are only responsible for raising $750,000 and I have given you a contact list and a strategy. It will be fun, wait and see!"

"Jan, what is this guy thinking? Of the $8,000,000 we need, according to Mike's plan, the staff are responsible for raising over half of it!"

"Calm down, Amy. It is not going to be that bad. You are so very passionate about what we do here that I cannot imagine it will be difficult for you and your staff to meet your goal of $750,000. As an incentive, the board also indicated any staff member reaching their goal on time would receive a one-time bonus equal to 5 percent of their base pay. As an additional incentive, any funds raised in excess of your assigned goals will be matched in your operating budget next year for program 'extras.' I am really excited about this bonus structure the board approved and I know all of you will be anxious to cash those bonus checks!"

The following conversation takes place between facility director Amy Green and education director Amber Smith three months later after a staff meeting.

"I don't know how Mike is doing it but he is already at almost 50 percent of his goal for this capital campaign and we are only three months into it."

"I know, Amber, I not only don't know how he does it but where does he find the time? I realize his full time job is development but he doesn't seem to have slacked off in his grant writing or planning for the annual operating campaign."

"I think I will follow him around for a week and take notes on what he does. Maybe I can pick up a few pointers. Want me to take a few notes for you too, Amy?"

"Sure why not. I'm only at 10 percent of my goal and will take any help I can get!"

One month later at a meeting between CEO, Jan Damon, and development director, Mike Moran.

"Mike I don't know how you are doing it but your success in the capital campaign is absolutely phenomenal! Care to share the secret of your success?"

"I told you, Jan, it's having a plan and working your plan. I talked with our treasurer, Tom Mayer last night after meeting with the volunteers and he said they are at 35 percent of their goal. It's not quite where I wanted them to be but I guess those volunteers don't get as excited about a plaque as I do about a 5 percent bonus. All total, it looks like we are at 50 percent of our goal. Oh, Tom said to call him about some promising news from one of the banks."

Returning to her office, Jan calls Treasurer Tom Mayer.

"Hi Tom, Mike Moran mentioned you had some promising news from one of the banks."

"Glad you called,Jan. I was at a charity golf tournament with Andy Banks last Friday. He is the chief loan officer at the new First Community Bank here in town. He said he could probably get his loan committee to approve us for a construction loan at prime once we have pledges equal to 90 percent of our goal. Since they are new in town, they seem to be a little more flexible than the bankers that have been here a while."

"That is terrific news, Tom. Mike told me today we were already at 50 percent of our goal after only four months of the campaign. I will give Andy a call and see if he can improve on his 90 percent offer."

KNOWLEDGE CHECK

1. Which is accurate of We Care?

   a. The board initially authorized the CEO to solicit consultants to conduct a fundraising campaign.
   b. We Care is not a 501(c)(3).
   c. At a recent meeting, the board of directors approved plans to expand the existing shelter to house an additional 20 residents and to construct a new shelter in the southern portion of the county.
   d. The CEO prepares the capital campaign plan.

Later that day Jan calls Andy and together they come up with a plan for a construction loan when 75 percent of the goal has been reached and with 25 percent of those pledges collected.

At that week's board meeting, Jan is authorised to have First Community Bank draw up the paper work as soon as the 75 percent pledge and 25 percent collection goals have been met. The morning following the meeting, Jan meets with Mike Moran and CFO, Brian Michaels, to tell them the news.

"Brian, I need you and Mike to work together to get the exact results of the campaign to date and then stay on top of them for the next few weeks. Brian, I want you to get the loan package from Andy at First Community and start getting the paperwork together. As soon as we hit the 75 percent-25 percent level, I want to get the papers signed and to the bank."

"Sure thing, Jan. Mike, can you meet me in my office in a few minutes so we can get started on this? I need a minute with Jan first."

"What is it, Brian?"

"Jan, I don't want to be negative or anything but I am a little concerned with the quality of some of these pledges Mike is bringing in."

"What do you mean Brian? I thought Mike was at 75 percent or more of his goal."

"I think he is but he is not getting me the pledge information on a regular basis. The last time I got paperwork from him was two months ago. Based on that information, we were only at 15 percent of our goal. All I have to go on is what he says. Not only that, but I am not seeing a lot of checks coming in with these pledges. I know we are giving donors a 5-year payment option but aren't they supposed to be making the first payment with their pledge?"

"Yes, Brian, we are supposed to be getting either the entire payment or the first payment at the time of the pledge. When you talk with Mike, ask him if he wants you to send any friendly reminder notices to those donors that have not made their first payment. Also, tell him I would like to see the latest donor status list by the first of next week. Maybe he simply needs a little push to get his paperwork complete."

"Okay, Jan. If this doesn't work, you get to talk to him the next time."

"It is a deal, Brian."

The next Monday morning, Mike hands Jan the latest donor status report and tells her he also gave Brian all of the paperwork he had let pile up over the last two months. Mike tells Jan they are able to meet the 75 percent-25 percent level based on the latest information.

Later that day in CFO, Brian Michaels' office.

"Brian, Mike tells me we are at the 75 percent-25 percent level we need to apply for the interim financing. How soon can you get the application together and to the bank?"

"Well, I need a few days to go over Mike's reports and determine the accuracy of the information. Then it will be a few more days before I and my staff can get things input and review the first run GL and financials."

"Listen, Brian. You know how important it is not only for staff but the community that we get these capital projects going as soon as possible. Is there any way you can get things done quicker? Can you simply use Mike's information as is and then check it out later after you have sent the loan application to the bank?"

"Jan, I would rather not use information I have not at least reviewed and I really prefer to determine how accurate the information is before I use it to update our books. Since we will be using the interim financials and the pledge reports as part of what we give the bank, I would like to make sure they are as complete and accurate as possible."

"I realize you want things to be 'perfect' Brian; but, this time I am going to override you because we simply cannot wait to get these projects going. Now, with this directive, how soon can you get things together for the bank?"

"Providing everyone leaves me alone for a few days and there are no emergencies, I should be able to get the records up to date and the interim financial statements completed by Thursday morning. Once that's done, I can get the application completed and take it and the financial and pledge information to the bank, say, by Friday."

"It would really be better if you could get everything done and to the bank by Wednesday afternoon. Andy Banks told me their loan committee meets on Mondays and if we don't get the information to him early enough in the week we have to wait until the next loan committee meeting. I will even approve the overtime pay for your staff to get things done by Wednesday."

"Okay, I get the message 'sacrifice accuracy for timeliness'. Never mind, Jan. I am a little disturbed but I will get over it."

"That's great, Brian. I knew I could count on you. I will let the executive committee know we are finally on our way to getting the capital plan financed."

Thanking him, Jan heads to the break room and runs into Carl Jones, the partner on the We Care audit engagement.

"Hey there, Carl. Did I forget we have an appointment today?"

"No, nothing like that. I needed to drop off my pledge card and payment and decided to stop in to see if Brian had time to see me. Year end is coming up next month and I want to go over a few things with him we plan to do differently this year. He had to deal with an irate donor first and pointed me in the direction of the coffee while he took care of things with the donor."

"Oh, an irate donor. That doesn't sound like a very good way to start a week. Poor Brian. Make sure he gets a chance to update you on our capital campaign. I got the word from Brian a few minutes ago; we have what we need to complete the loan application for the bank. It looks as if we will be able to get the financing finalized in the next few weeks. Needless to say, this capital campaign has all of us going in circles right now. See you later, Carl."

"Bye, Jan."

Three weeks later, Brian Michaels walks into Jan's office with an armful of print outs and a grim look on his face.

"Brian, what is going on with you? I know it's getting close to year end and your days are pretty full getting everything ready for the auditors. You have been through year end before, so surely things cannot be that bad."

"I wish I could say things were fine but I think I would be lying if I did. Jan, have you had a chance to look over those donor status reports Mike prepared? If not, do you have a few minutes for me to talk over my thoughts on them?"

"Sure, Brian. Have a seat and talk away."

"Remember a few weeks ago when I mentioned my concerns about the lack of paperwork and differences in the results? I spent some time today going over what Mike left for me and I think I have more questions now than I did then."

"Take a look at this list. Do you recognize the names of some of these major gift donors? Have you ever heard of Acme Consulting, Zippy Cleaning, or Basha's Boots? These are $25,000 5-year pledges and I have never heard of them. I did an Internet search and could find nothing on them either. Oh, I forgot, there is a Basha's Boots somewhere in west Texas but that address is not what is on the pledge card. Speaking of pledge cards, you would not believe how incomplete some of them are. I am going to have to have someone on my staff try and locate the addresses and phone numbers for these people. Year-end is next week. I am nowhere near meeting my campaign goal ..."

"Brian, Brian. Calm down."

"That is easy for you to say, Jan, but this information is what I used to prepare the interim financials that we gave to the bank with the loan application. We also gave the bank this donor status report. They used this information when they approved our loan two weeks ago and we are scheduled to take our first draw next week."

"Let me guess, Brian, this is where you tell me 'I told you so'!"

EXERCISES

1. Are there any potential fraud risks in this case? If so, what are they?

2. How should the fraud triangle be considered by the auditor of We Care?

3. What type of preliminary audit procedures should be considered in this situation?

4. What type of other audit procedures should be considered in this situation?

5. If you were the CFO, what would you do?

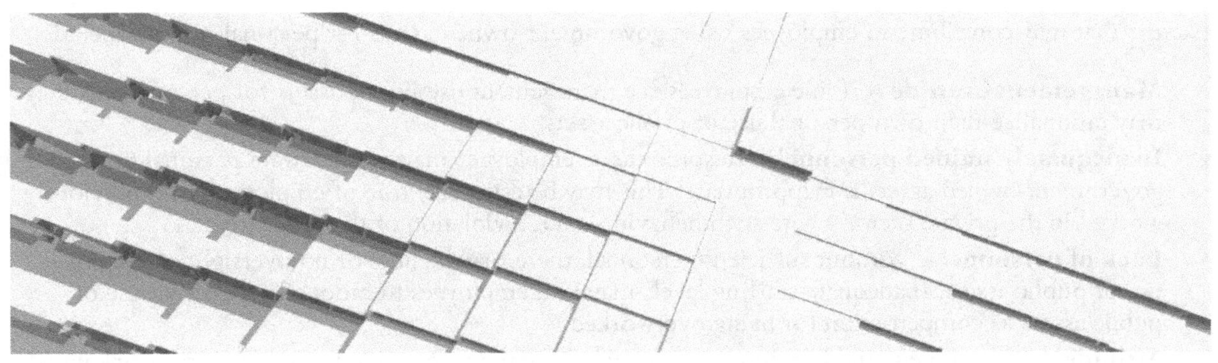

Chapter 7

Case 7: Personal Use of Public Assets

Learning Objectives

After completing this chapter, you should be able to do the following:

- Determine the importance of identifying the environment in which a fictitious governmental organization operates and how the operating environment may affect the development and execution of policies and procedures.
- Identify capitalization policies and inventory procedures of a fictitious governmental organization.

Before We Start

In many governmental organizations an attitude may be present that encourages personal use of government assets. This may be as insignificant as management tolerating personal use of copiers or as egregious as operating a personal business from the fire station. Such situations may not likely result in material misstatements due to misappropriation of assets. However, such personal use of public assets violates the public trust.

Factors that may contribute to employees using government-owned assets for personal reasons include:

- **Management override** – If line employees see management use public assets for personal use, they may rationalize their own personal use of public assets.
- **Inadequately trained personnel** – In some cases, employees may not be aware personal use of government-owned assets is inappropriate. This may be especially true of employees who previously worked in the private sector where such behavior is not a violation of the public trust.
- **Lack of personnel** – Without sufficient personnel, there may be little or no oversight of employee use of public assets. Inadequate staffing levels may lead employees to rationalize personal use of public assets as compensation for being overworked.
- **Attitude** – Management and line employees may believe they are entitled to use government-owned assets for their personal use.
- **Lack of controls** – There may be little benefit to the cost of controls over the personal use of public assets. This may lead many governments to have few, if any, controls over personal use of public assets.

Assets subject to personal use include the following:

- Computers
- Cell phones
- Vehicles
- Audio-visual equipment
- Buildings
- Others

THE CASE

River City is a medium-sized city with operations centrally located at City Hall Complex as well as several off-site locations. Off-site operations include two city parks, three fire stations, two police substations, a city-owned and operated garage, and the water and sewer plant.

Your firm has been selected to perform the audit of the financial statements and this is the first year of a five-year audit contract. Because the city spent $2,000,000 received from the U.S. Department of Transportation for widening Main Street, the engagement is subject to Government Auditing Standards and a single audit is required. As part of the preliminary audit planning, the in-charge, Brent Mullins, has obtained the following information related to capital assets from the director of finance, Kristen Davis.

River City Selected Capital Asset Policies
The city's capitalization threshold is $5,000 for vehicles, furniture and fixtures, and equipment. For buildings, the capitalization threshold is $25,000 and for infrastructure assets the capitalization threshold is $50,000.
All capitalized assets are tagged or marked in some way to indicate city ownership. Asset tags are alpha coded by department, pre-numbered, and used sequentially by the respective departments.
Assets not subject to the city's capitalization policy are not required to be tagged. However, all departments are required to maintain records for any capital asset having a serial number.
The IT department maintains all computer and computer-related equipment. All computer and computer-related equipment is identified and tracked using their own departmental asset identification and tagging system.
Each department is required to take an annual inventory of its tagged capital assets. The finance department provides each department with asset count sheets that are generated by the city's asset management system.
Non tagged capital assets are also required to be inventoried every year. Because no central records exist for these assets, each department uses their own inventory management form(s). A copy of each departmental inventory is forwarded to the finance department once complete. The finance department reviews these lists for purposes of updating insurance coverage on non-tagged assets.
All tagged capital assets, in all locations, are insured under a blanket contents insurance policy.
Non tagged capital assets are insured upon request by the applicable department head.
Tagged capital assets not kept in city buildings (that is, vehicles, heavy equipment, boats, and the like) are insured as separately listed property on the appropriate insurance policy.
The city has a formal written policy prohibiting the use of city assets for personal purposes. The only exception to this is *de minimis* personal use of computers and cellular phones. *De minimis* use is not defined in the policy.

Because this is the first year your firm has audited River City, engagement partner, Robin Weaver, determines it would be appropriate to observe the annual capital asset inventory for the fire, police, parks, and information technology departments.

KNOWLEDGE CHECK

1. Which is accurate of River City?

    a. The city does not have formal written capital asset policies.
    b. River City is a medium-sized city with operations centrally located at City Hall Complex as well as several off-site locations.
    c. Off-site operations consist of one park and one police substation.
    d. River City has had the same audit firm for many years.

The following conversation takes place during the capital asset inventory at one of the parks between staff auditor, Doug Carnes, and recreation coordinator, Becky Peterson.

"Becky, thanks for getting me this copy of your count sheet. It will make it a lot easier for me to follow what you're doing here."

"I would gladly do anything if it meant I could get you out of here faster. I can't believe you want to watch me count basketballs and finger paint."

"Come on now, Becky, be a sport. I won't be here that long. Where do you start, with the big items or the little things?"

"Let's start with what is here in the building because it is 110 degrees outside. Maybe by the time we finish inside, it will have cooled off enough to look over what is in the storage shed."

A little while later.

"Okay, Doug. We are done in here it looks like."

"Okay but what about these things you did not check yet? What about the LCD projector and digital camera at the bottom of the list?"

"They are not here now but I know where they are. The digital camera is in the director's car and the LCD projector is at City Hall."

"What are they doing in those places? They belong to the parks department."

"Yeah, they do but the director's daughter's dance recital was this past weekend and she used the camera to take pictures at the recital. I think the LCD projector was used for a presentation at the P&Z meeting last week and we have not had a chance to get it."

Doug makes a note on his count sheet to follow up on the two items.

Knowledge Check

2. Which is accurate of River City's policies related to capital assets?

    a. For buildings, the capitalization threshold is $2,000.
    b. The city's capitalization threshold is $5,000 for vehicles, furniture and fixtures, and equipment.
    c. For infrastructure assets the capitalization threshold is $5,000.
    d. Assets not subject to the city's capitalization policy are required to be tagged.

Later in the storage shed.

"Now this is the scary part of the inventory. I hope you can handle it Doug."

Wiping cobwebs out of his hair, Doug says "No problem, Becky. Lead the way."

"Now this is strange. The volleyball equipment is supposed to be over here next to the swim blocks instead of propped up next to the riding mower. The public works supervisor and I have the only keys to this shed. I haven't been in here since we put things up three weeks ago after the employee picnic. That's why I know the volleyball equipment is not where I left it."

"Well, let's count what we need to and get back into the AC, okay Becky?"

Meanwhile, Brent Mullins is observing the inventory at the police department being conducted by Lieutenant Buzz Linder.

Opening the gun storage locker, Buzz says "We keep all the assault weapons in here except for those that are assigned to vehicles and specific individuals."

Buzz leads Brent around the room while they count the various weapons and agree them to the various count sheets.

"Now, in this room we keep all the various electronic equipment we use for surveillance and stake outs as well as training. See, here are the TVs, DVD recorders, cameras and lenses.. .wait a minute. Where is the new duplicating equipment we bought last month?"

"What do you mean Bu22? Is something missing?"

"It's probably checked out to one of the units but it is our new DVD copier set-up. Last year, the Chief decided we could make our own training videos and market them to other agencies to bring in some extra revenue. We couldn't keep up with the demand so we got some great state-of-the-art high quality equipment that would let us mass produce the DVDs as well as USB drives. I'll check the logs later to see who has the equipment."

Brent makes a note to follow up on these items at a later date. Leaving the police department, Brent runs into Robin Weaver in the City Hall parking lot.

Knowledge Check

3. Which is accurate of River City's policies related to capital assets?

   a. The IT department maintains all computer and computer-related equipment.
   b. Computer and computer-related equipment is neither identified nor tracked.
   c. Asset tags are pre-numbered but do not have to be used sequentially.
   d. Asset tags are not alpha coded by department.

"Hi there, Robin, I wasn't aware you were coming out here today."

"Don't worry, Brent. I saw the city manager at Rotary this morning and he asked me to stop by and see him this afternoon. It was a very interesting meeting but I do not want to stand here in this 100 degree parking lot to talk about it. Let's meet in my office early tomorrow morning before you head out here."

"Okay, Robin, I will see you in the AM."

The next morning in the office of Robin Weaver, partner on the River City audit engagement.

"Thanks for coming in this early, Brent. I really did not want to talk about this at City Hall yesterday. The reason the city manager wanted to see me was to ask about some of the city's policies and procedures. I told him we had already looked at a number of them and were now evaluating them for audit planning purposes."

"Did he have anything specific in mind?"

"We spent a lot of time talking about personal use of city-owned assets. Apparently, when he worked for the county, they had a big scandal in a few departments about this. The state attorney even got involved at one point because some of it related to grant purchased assets and facilities."

"Wow, sure sounds like one fun forensic accounting opportunity. What is he concerned about here in River City?"

"He seems to think a lot of equipment and such is being used for personal purposes and it is not confined to employees. Last weekend he was at Commissioner Burns' house for a picnic with a few of the region's movers and shakers. While there, he got the nickel tour of the commissioner's house and could not help but notice a few things."

"Oh yeah, like what? Police cruisers in the garage or a brass pole instead of a staircase?"

"Come on, Brent. I have a hard time handling your sense of humor on only one cup of coffee. He did say he was almost certain the golf cart shuttling guests from the street to the house belonged to public works. Another thing he thought he saw was an asset tag on the side of the big screen television in the commissioner's study."

"What does he want us to do about this? Did he say anything else?"

"Although he was very disturbed by what he might have seen at Commissioner Burns' house, he is also concerned about what is going on at City Hall as well. According to him, when he walks around the various city offices, he sees a lot of employees web surfing, sending emails, and visiting social media sites. He is not real sure how much of this is happening and if it would fall under their *de minimis* provision or not. But, he is concerned because he thinks some employees end up working overtime because they are too busy with personal business during working hours."

"It sounds like we need to expand some of our audit procedures. I can't believe none of us thought of this kind of thing when we had the brainstorming session last month. What do you think we should do?"

KNOWLEDGE CHECK

4. Which is accurate of River City's policies related to capital assets?

   a. All departments are required to maintain records for any capital asset having a serial number.
   b. Assets not subject to the city's capitali2ation policy are required to be tagged.
   c. The city does not identify any of its assets using a tag system.
   d. The finance department maintains all capital asset records.

EXERCISES

1. What specific audit procedures could be done to determine if any city-owned assets are being used for non-public purposes?

2. What would you do if you were the partner on this audit engagement and why?

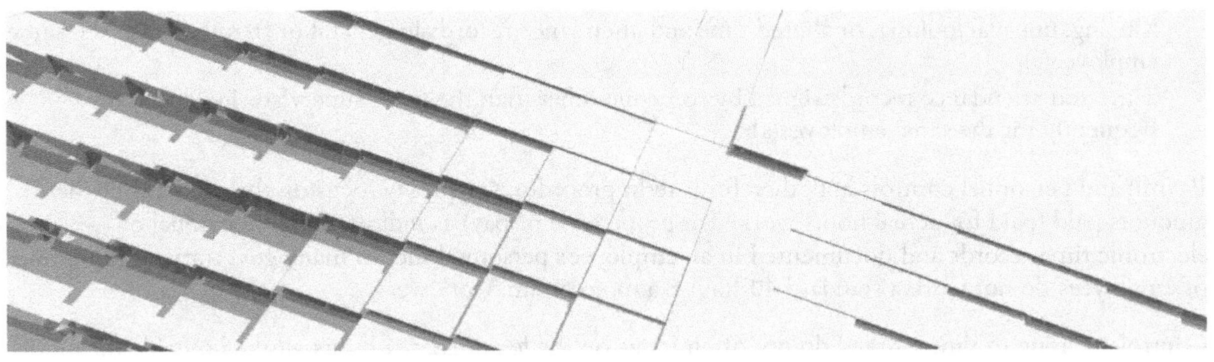

Chapter 8

CASE 8: FICTITIOUS EMPLOYEES

LEARNING OBJECTIVES

After completing this chapter, you should be able to do the following:

- Determine how audit procedures may or may not detect fraudulent personnel in the audit of a fictitious not-for-profit (NFP) entity.
- Identify how personnel policies and procedures of a fictitious NFP can be circumvented and lead to possible fraud or abuse

BEFORE WE START

In many NFP entities, salaries and benefits represent the largest natural expense categories. Employees of NFPs are often paid less than their counterparts in the private sector which may lead some employees to rationalize misappropriation of assets as compensation for their low salary levels.

NFPs with offsite locations often create opportunities for fraud that are exacerbated when these offsite locations lack adequate or qualified personnel. In addition to these personnel issues, management may provide limited or no oversight of the operations and personnel at offsite locations.

Indicators of personnel fraud include the following:

- Unusual or second-party endorsements on payroll check images
- Employees without the usual withholdings related to employer provided or offered benefits (that is, insurance, retirement, savings bonds, and so on)

- Missing, unusual looking, or altered time and attendance records in general or frequently for the same employee(s)
- Time and attendance records signed by someone other than the usual supervisor in general or frequently for the same employee(s)

Payroll and personnel controls and, therefore, audit procedures, typically focus on the accuracy of the amounts paid (paid for actual hours worked at proper rate of pay) as indicated on the manual or electronic time records and documented in an employee's personnel file. In many governments, a number of employees do not work a standard 40-hour 8 a.m. to 5 p.m. work week.

Controls relating to time worked do not often focus on the legitimacy of hours worked outside the regular work day or work week. In many governments, the approval of an employee's supervisor is evidence of legitimate time worked when the supervisor may not be personally aware this is the case.

THE CASE

Smart Kids is a 501(c)(3) located in a large metropolitan area in a southwestern state. They have been in existence for 25 years and currently provide tutoring services to over 2,500 elementary and middle school students. Services are provided to any student who qualifies for the tutoring program and a sliding scale fee structure is in place. Amounts charged for tutoring services are based on household income and do not cover the entire cost of providing the service. State and federal Department of Education and Department of Health and Human Services grants and fundraising efforts augment tutoring revenues.

Most tutoring services are provided at 30 elementary and middle school libraries, but some tutoring services are provided at the Smart Kids' office. Regardless of location, students having scheduled tutoring sessions pay for tutoring services at the beginning of each week while drop-in students pay for services at the beginning of each session they attend. For certain at-risk students or for schools in economically depressed areas, the applicable area school board pays for the tutoring services for qualifying low income students. Smart Kids bills the participating school boards monthly and in arrears for these services.

A part-time program assistant is assigned to each school location where tutoring services are provided. Education majors from the local university are hired as part-time tutors at school locations. Tutoring services provided at the Smart Kids' office are provided by a full-time program assistant who is assisted by part-time college students who act as tutors. In some cases, the program coordinator provides tutoring services when program assistants are unavailable either at the Smart Kids' office or school sites.

KNOWLEDGE CHECK

1. Which is accurate of Smart Kids?

   a. Students having scheduled tutoring sessions pay for tutoring services at the beginning of each week.

   b. Most tutoring services are provided at the Smart Kids office.

   c. Amounts charged for tutoring services are not based on household income.

   d. All tutoring services are provided at off-site locations.

Program assistants assigned to each school location are authorized to hire as many college students as needed to meet state mandated teacher-student coverage ratios. However, a lengthy background investigation must be completed before any employee is allowed to work with the students. In some cases, it may take up to six weeks from the time of application until the background investigation is complete. This lag often leads to shortages in tutoring personnel at the school locations.

To compensate for this, and to maintain statutory teacher-student ratios, school program assistants are allowed to use "day labor" for up to 20 hours per week and for no more than four weeks in any calendar year. Day laborers are usually friends of the university students working as tutors and are paid outside the payroll system. Day laborers are simply set up as vendors in the accounts payable system needing only a vendor set up form rather than a full personnel package and related background investigation and health screening.

The following conversation occurs between A lice Goodings, program coordinator, and Fred Smith, a school program assistant.

"Listen, Alice. I am not sure if you have heard or not but my wife and I have separated and things are not looking good for the long term. I'm staying with a friend and Janice and the kids are in the house. If you need to get hold of me after hours, call my cell because I am not sure Janice will pass on any messages to me."

"I am truly sorry to hear about you andjanice, Fred. I sure hope you two are able to work things out."

"Thanks, Alice, I appreciate your concern and kind words. Financially, things are a mess right now and probably will be for the next few months. We both want to try counseling but our health insurance does not cover marital counseling. If I was a drug addict, they would pay for drug counseling but they won't cover counseling to keep a family together. Go figure. Do you think there is any way I could have my annual performance evaluation early? I am really going to need any extra cash I can get."

"About the only thing Smart Kids can do to help is offer you a small short-term loan. Those HR folks do not let anything happen outside of their time schedule, which means you will have to wait five more months for your annual performance evaluation like the rest of us. I'm really sorry, Fred."

"That's okay, Alice. If you think of anything else, let me know."

A few weeks later, Fred and two other schoolprogram assistants, Hank Wallace and Tim Cole, stop for lunch after the monthly all-staff meeting. Fred is telling Hank and Tim about his family situation.

"Aw man, Fred. This is just awful. I can't believe you andjanice are not together anymore. You two were high school sweethearts, right?"

"Yeah, Hank, something like that. Not being able to see my girls every day is killing me. Janice won't even think about us getting back together until we can get counseling and..."

Tim interrupts saying "Why is it women think counseling is the answer to all of life's problems. When will they figure out guys do not talk about feelings? My ex tried to get me to do that stuff too and I told her 'no way, Jack'."

"Don't listen to him, Fred. I say go for the counseling if you really want a chance of getting back together with Janice. What's the hold up, anyway?"

"Money, Hank, money. Our health insurance plan does not cover marriage counseling and money is very tight right now what with us maintaining two households and all. I asked Alice if there was anything I could do to get my annual performance evaluation done early, but she said HR will not go for it."

"That is too bad, Fred. I could spot you a little if you needed it but with two kids in college it's pretty tight for us right now, too. How come you always seem to have money, Tim? You support three kids and four ex-wives."

"That really hurts, man. It's four kids and three ex-wives. I am really hurt you don't remember your almost best buddy's family situations. Fred, walk with me when we leave this joint and I'll give you a few financial pointers."

KNOWLEDGE CHECK

2. Which is accurate of Fred's personal situation?

    a. Fred's wife is insisting she and Fred go through counseling.
    b. Fred's children need braces for their teeth.
    c. Fred has not discussed his personal situation with anyone associated with Smart Kids.
    d. Fred's personal situation has not changed since he began working for Smart Kids.

On the way to their cars, Tim pulls Fred aside.

"Listen, Fred. There is a real easy way for you to snag a little extra money for yourself compliments of Smart Kids. All you have to do is dummy up some day laborer paperwork and before you know it, you will be having 40 or so extra paid hours a week."

"I'm not sure I know what you mean, Tim?"

"You know how HR lets us fill in with day laborers when we need to meet teacher-student ratios? All you have to do is 'create' yourself a couple of these day laborers every month or two and you take home the checks for the bogus day laborers."

"How do you know this works, Tim?"

"Man are you naive. I do this all the time when I get a little short or want to buy myself something special. I love my job, man, but they do not pay us worth a darn, and I have four kids and three ex-wives to support. Rest assured, I'm not smart enough to have figured this out on my own."

"Hey, do you remember Joe Francis from a few years back? He's the one who told me about this scam. According tojoe, this has been going on for years here at Smart Kids!"

"Not to sound preachy, Tim, but the fact it has been going on for years doesn't make it right. Besides, what do you do for a social security number and an address?"

"You can make up a social security number or you can find them on the web. As for addresses, pick any of those apartment complexes out by the university and your dummy employee is going to look like our real college kid employees."

"I don't know Tim. AH of this sounds like a lot of risk for not much reward."

"Listen, Fred. You think about this over the weekend and let me know if you need any additional pointers. While you think it over, think about this. See my new car over there? How do you think I can afford it?"

"I never really thought about it Tim. You always have a nice car."

"I'm making the payments using paychecks from one of my dummy employees. This month I have three dummies going because one of my kids needs money for a football camp. You are the math major, how many marital counseling sessions do you think you could pay for with this scam? My only advice for you is to keep it simple and don't let anyone know what you're doing."

"Thanks for the info, Tim. I certainly have a lot to think about over the weekend."

Knowledge Check

3. Which is accurate of Tim's day laborer fraud schemes?

   a. Tim only recently began his day laborer fraud scheme.
   b. Tim's day labor fraud schemes help support his four children and three ex-wives.
   c. Fred has to convince Tim to share details regarding his day laborer fraud schemes.
   d. Tim is the mastermind for the day laborer fraud schemes.

Monday morning, Fred calls Agnes Taylor the retired bookkeeping teacher who has been the accountant for Smart Kids since its inception.

"Hi Agnes, this is Fred Smith, the program assistant for Pleasantville Middle."

"Good morning, Fred. What can I do for you?"

"I am not sure if I really should be talking to you about this but I have to talk to someone. Can we meet for coffee somewhere one morning this week?"

"Sure thing, Fred. Can you meet me about 10:00 this morning at the little shop in the lobby of the building next door?"

Later, over coffee, Fred tells Agnes about the dummy day-laborer scam in very general terms.

"Where did you hear this, Fred?"

"I would rather not say, Agnes. You only need to know it was from someone with some experience in this organization."

"I can appreciate your discretion. How did you come to find out about this anyway?"

"Well, um, its, um. Oh Agnes,Janice and I have separated and she will not even talk reconciliation until we get counseling. I need to find some way to pay for counseling because our insurance doesn't cover it. Someone offered me this dummy employee scam as a way to get some quick extra cash."

"Now Fred, I'm real sorry to hear about you and Janice. I wish you would have come to me first. I could have told you to go see those folks over at Healthy Families. They have some low cost counseling services as part of a grant they have from DHHS."

"Really? Why have I never heard about it?"

"Silly goose, probably because you didn't need their services before. Now what do you want me to do about this other thing?"

"Well, is there any way you can figure out whether this is really going on or not? I mean, if it really has been going on for all these years it seems like someone would have noticed something. Our auditors are supposed to find this kind of stuff, right?"

"You've given me something to think about Fred. Now, you quit your worrying and let me handle things from here on out. You make sure you give those sweet girls of yours a hug from me, okay?"

Knowledge Check

4. After learning of Tim's day laborer fraud schemes, who does Fred approach about the situation?

   a. Agnes Taylor.
   b. The local police.
   c. The board of directors.
   d. The CEO of Smart Kids.

EXERCISES

1. What would you do if you were the accountant for Smart Kids?

2. What specific procedures can be done to determine if the dummy employee scheme is actually being perpetrated?

3. What factors contributed to the dummy employee scheme? What procedures or controls could have prevented this situation?

4. Why might the auditor not have found the dummy employee scheme during prior audit engagements?

Chapter 9

CASE 9: MISAPPROPRIATION OF ASSETS

LEARNING OBJECTIVES

After completing this chapter, you should be able to do the following:

- Identify how procurement policies of a fictitious governmental organization can be circumvented and lead to possible fraud.
- Determine the effect technical expertise plays in the development and execution of procurement policies in a fictitious governmental organization.

BEFORE WE START

Governmental organizations typically focus controls more on cash receipts than on cash disbursements in order to prevent, deter, or detect the misappropriation of cash. Fraud schemes to misappropriate cash can also occur when an entity pays for goods or services it does not receive. Factors contributing to this particular situation include the following:

- Highly technical transactions
- Insufficient number of trained personnel
- Lack of personnel, or lack of trained personnel, in support functions.

Typical situations that might indicate the existence of procurement or contracting fraud include the following:

- Unusual vendor names and addresses
- Copies of invoices, purchase orders, or receiving documents rather than original documents
- Orders for materials and supplies already on hand in sufficient quantities or that are scheduled for disposal or discontinued use due to obsolescence
- Orders for materials and supplies not consistent with the operations or mission of the organization
- Delivery addresses not part of the purchaser's physical locations
- Payments to vendors not on approved vendor lists
- Signature of management or supervisory personnel on documents typically signed by subordinate personnel
- Suppliers and contractors receiving significant amounts of business from the organization

The Case

Bellview County is a large rural county located in a large but sparsely populated state in the northwest. The county is largely rural, except for the county seat, and the majority of residents are involved directly or indirectly with the agricultural business. Because the county is large and many residents do not reside in villages, towns, or cities, service delivery is difficult. Extremely long and cold winters also complicate county operations as well as service delivery.

Over the years, the county has used various forms of transportation to increase service delivery efficiency and effectiveness. For example, all-terrain vehicles, snow mobiles, and personal water craft are used by various county departments including the sheriff, fire marshal, and public works. A number of storage facilities are strategically located throughout the county to house these items.

Ten years ago, the county received a grant from the state to purchase a helicopter to be used by the sheriff s department in search and rescue operations. The grant-funded helicopter became indispensable to the county and an additional helicopter was purchased by the county three years ago. The oldest helicopter, "Black Widow," is housed at the fire station located in the southern part of the county and used by the fire department. "King Cobra," the newest helicopter, is housed at the sheriff s compound near the county annex in the northern part of the county and used exclusively by the sheriff s department.

Knowledge Check

1. Which is accurate of Bellview County?

    a. Bellview County is located in a southern state.
    b. Bellview County is largely urban.
    c. The majority of the residents of Bellview County are involved in the agricultural business.
    d. Bellview County received grant funding to purchase both of its helicopters.

The following discussion occurs over dinner in the south fire station one winter evening.

"Hey, Mary Jo, what have you been doing outside? It has to be five below without the wind chill."

"Make that 15 below with a wind chill of minus 40, Stan. I had to go out and check on the Black Widow. She is getting a little old for a storm this severe. The last thing I need is for her to blow a gasket on me when I'm up there battling 80 mile per hour gusts."

"You better watch out, Mary Jo, you will spoil the old girl. She is a real tough old bird and will probably outlast King Cobra."

"You're probably right on that one, Stan. She really is a classic even if she is high maintenance."

"One of these days the commission is going to decide that it would be cheaper to replace her than it is to maintain her."

"Shut your mouth, Stan Bridges! I'll call the sheriff and have him arrest you for treason if you say something like that again."

"Okay, Mary Jo *Carpenter*. You go on and call Sheriff Paul Carpenter. I bet he won't lift a finger to save your favorite bucket of bolts."

"I know he still hasn't forgiven me for spilling the beans to Mom about the baby coming. It happened six months ago for goodness' sake! You would think he would have let up by now, especially because the baby is almost here."

A month later in the county accounts payable department.

"Kate, how about lunch?"

"Thanks, Janice, but I really need to get these invoices entered before 3:00. We need to cut checks first thing tomorrow and if I take time out for lunch, I won't finish in time."

"Why do you have so many invoices this week? Did the commissioners increase everyone's budget or what?"

"No, we wish, though. Most of these came over from the sheriff s office. Things backed up over there these last few weeks because he was home with his new baby girl."

"Maybe I can give you a hand with these now and then we could both go to lunch later. Let me have half of them."

"Thanks, Janice. Here you go."

A few minutes later Janice looks up from an invoice and frowns.

"Kate, I don't know how you do this. None of these things they buy over in the sheriff s office make a lot of sense to me. I can't tell if this invoice is for tear gas or bullets. Look at this one, if it didn't say 'helicopter parts,' I would never have known what we were buying."

"I know, Janice. I have been in AP almost five years and still don't recognize a lot of what we buy. At least I am pretty familiar with most of the vendors now which helps some. About the time I think I really know the vendors we use, the commissioners approve something new and I have a whole new batch of vendors to learn."

"You know, Janice, we must have added ten new vendors when we bought that new helicopter back three years ago or so. One for this kind of part, another for that kind of part, three for maintenance, and so on and so on. Thank goodness someone over in the sheriff s office knows what all these things are we keep buying."

"I am finished over here, Kate. You ready for lunch now?"

A few weeks later in the office of Paul Carpenter, sheriff.

"Come on, Paul. I want to go and see my new niece. You promised me if I brought the pizza, I could see the baby tonight."

"Maryjo, give me a few minutes, okay? I need to make a few more calls and then I'm done for the night."

KNOWLEDGE CHECK

2. Which is accurate of the helicopters owned by Bellview County?

    a. Black Widow is Bellview County's oldest helicopter.
    b. King Cobra is Bellview County's oldest helicopter.
    c. The Bellview Fire Department is responsible for maintenance on King Cobra.
    d. Bellview County currently owns three helicopters.

While Sheriff Carpenter makes his phone calls, Mary Jo starts to straighten the paperwork piled on the edges of his desk. Glancing at the top of one pile, she notices an invoice for helicopter parts and laughs.

"Hey big brother, what is up with the helicopter parts? Did the big, bad King Cobra get a boo boo?"

"Cut it out, Maryjo. That helicopter is going to be the death of me yet. Right now, I wish we had never bought it."

"What do you mean, Paul?"

"It seems like we are always buying parts for it. One week, it's a new rear rotor blade, the next week a new windshield and on and on like that. I don't remember Black Widow being this high maintenance when she was a younger bird."

"She wasn't, Paul, and King Cobra should not be either. He is top of the line, or at least he was three years ago. In fact, one of the big things the manufacturer promotes about that model is the low maintenance cost. If you let me take a look at the maintenance logs tomorrow, I'll see if I can find anything."

"That sounds great, Maryjo. Come on, let's go see my new best girl."

Two days later Mary Jo calls her brother, Sheriff Carpenter.

"Hi there, Paul. I got a chance to look at those maintenance logs on King Cobra we talked about the other night and I did not see anything out of line. You must have gotten one that was made on a Monday. Sorry about that, Big Brother."

"Thanks anyway for looking into it for me. I appreciate it."

Later that night when Mary Jo is exercising in the south station gym, she jumps off the treadmill and runs to get her cell phone.

"Come on, Paul. Be there for me..."

"This better be good, Mary Jo. We just got to sleep after walking the baby up and down the hall for two hours."

"It will be, Paul, I promise. The other day, I think you mentioned something about a windshield?"

"What in the world are you talking about, Maryjo? Which day? What windshield?"

"You were complaining about King Cobra being a money pit and I thought you said something about a new windshield."

"Ah, yeah, I guess I did. Seems like we replaced it two or three months ago. Why, what's wrong with that?"

"Nothing, Paul, except I did not see any mention of a new windshield in the maintenance logs when I looked at them. It was a pretty detailed log and I can't imagine something like a windshield would not have been noted."

"Listen, Maryjo, this is a little much for me right now as I am running on about three hours of sleep in the last week. See Kate in AP next time you are at the annex and pull the invoices for King's repairs."

"I'll do it in the morning on my way home."

The next morning in the accounts payable department.

"Hi there, Lieutenant Carpenter. How do you like being an aunt?"

"It is pretty great right now, Kate, because all I do is hold her when she is dry and fed. Ask me again when she hits her twos. I need to look at a few invoices for the sheriff. Can you log me on to the county-wide AP system?"

"Sure thing, Lieutenant. Here you are."

An hour later, Mary Jo hands Kate a list of five vendors and asks her to pull the paid files. After looking at the files for several hours and taking notes and making some copies, Mary Jo calls her brother and says she will see him at his house after work.

That evening in the sheriff's kitchen Mary Jo and Paul are talking.

"Look here, Paul. See this invoice, it's for engine parts, and this one here is for filters. Unless they have re-engineered King Cobra, these parts won't fit."

"What do you mean, MaryJo?"

"I am saying someone is buying helicopter parts for a helicopter you don't even own. Unfortunately, these invoices I copied look to be the tip of the iceberg. I only had time to go through the last few months thoroughly. One thing I did verify was that the windshield you mentioned was purchased but it doesn't fit King as it is for a two-seater and King is a four-seater."

"Wow, this is not looking good, Maryjo. What is your gut feel on this?"

"I would only say this to you, Big Brother, but it looks like someone is building a helicopter on your dime."

EXERCISES

1. What type of controls could be put in place to deter procurement-related fraud such as suspected in this case?

2. What type of centralized internal controls and procedures would be appropriate to determine if this type of situation was occurring?

3. What type of decentralized internal controls and procedures would be appropriate to determine if this type of situation was occurring?

4. What type of audit procedures would be appropriate to determine if this type of situation was occurring?

5. What would you do if you were the sheriff and why?

Chapter 10

Case 10: Donated Assets

Learning Objectives

After you have completed this chapter, you should be able to do the following:

- Identify how donated assets and capital assets in a fictitious not-for-profit (NFP) entity might be misappropriated.
- Identify fraud risks relating to opportunity in a fictitious NFP that might result in donated assets being misappropriated.

Before We Start

A number of NFPs have few, if any, controls over the receipt and disposition of donated assets. Often an NFP may not believe controls over donated assets are cost effective because they believe they do not receive assets of significant value. It is possible an NFP may in fact receive donated assets of significant value that are quickly and easily misappropriated due to the lack of controls.

Generally the types of property, plant, and equipment subject to misappropriation include physical assets that are

- small in size.
- high in value.
- high in consumer demand.
- easily convertible to cash.
- lacking in ownership identification.
- subject to personal or non-program use.
- susceptible to personal use or redirection.

THE CASE

Central Clinic, Inc. is a 501(c)(3) whose mission is to provide low cost health care to qualified individuals. Ostensibly, qualified individuals are those not eligible for Medicare or Medicaid and have a modified adjusted gross income (MAGI) less than 200 percent of the MAGI required by the Affordable Care Act. In reality, Central Clinic turns away no one in need of health care and, when appropriate, health insurance companies or health exchanges are billed for the health care services provided. Central Clinic was started in a rundown storefront fifteen years ago by a group of young, committed physicians. Today, the primary clinic is located near downtown Pleasantville and a small satellite office is located in the northern part of the county.

Currently, Central Clinic is managed on a day-to-day basis by the executive director. The executive director was appointed 14 months ago. In addition to the executive director, senior management consists of a director of operations and a director of finance. The director of operations is a licensed physician, board certified in emergency medicine, and has been with Central Clinic since its inception. Prior to being hired by the former executive director 18 months ago, the director of finance served as the budget director for the city of Pleasantville.

Central Clinic has developed an excellent reputation among the medical community for providing quality health care at little or no cost. To further Central Clinic's good work, a large number of physicians as well as area hospitals contribute their time, talent, and treasure to Central Clinic. As a result, contributions make up nearly 60 percent of the clinic's financial resources. Contributions consist of volunteer medical services, cash contributions, and donated equipment and supplies.

Central Clinic has a fixed asset policy which establishes a capitalization threshold for equipment at $2,500 and for buildings and improvements at $100,000. In the case of donated equipment, senior management is responsible for obtaining information from donors regarding the estimated fair value of donated items. The director of finance sends a thank you letter meeting the requirements of the IRS to donors within 30 days of the donation.

No asset identification system is used as most capitalized items consist of equipment with serial numbers. Because these assets are included as "scheduled property" on the insurance policy, the board feels no asset identification system is necessary. Additionally, the board does not believe annual inventories of fixed assets are necessary because most equipment is housed at the main clinic. Only a small amount of equipment is housed at the satellite clinic location.

The following discussion takes place near the end of the weekly Monday morning staff meeting. Presiding over the meeting is Executive Director Kirsten Lee. Present at the meeting are Director of Operations Sean Arthur, Director of Finance Lauren Gardner, and Office Manager Maggie Russell.

"Well, I think that is about all I had to cover. Does anyone else have something to discuss?"

"Kirsten, I got some good news at the Heart Association fundraiser the other night."

"What was it, Sean? Did you hear we were getting a multi-million dollar grant with no strings attached?"

"I said good news, not fantastic news, Kirsten. It seems County General is closing its drop-in clinic and is looking to find a few good homes for its equipment. I plan on finding out if this is true or rumor this morning and if it is true I will let you know what we need to do to get some of their equipment."

"That really would be good news, Sean. Make sure to keep me in the loop on things. As I recall, they received a large federal grant, oh probably no more than three years ago, to upgrade their diagnostic equipment. It would be really sweet if we could get our hands on some of it."

"Okay everybody, it is Monday and time to get to work. Sick people need us."

Knowledge Check

1. Which is accurate of Central Clinic's fixed asset policies?

   a. The board does not believe annual inventories of fixed assets are necessary because most equipment is housed at the main clinic.
   b. The board believes assets included as "scheduled property" on the insurance policy should be included in the asset identification system.
   c. An asset identification system is used as few capitalized items consist of equipment with serial numbers.
   d. The director of finance sends a thank you letter meeting the requirements of the IRS to donors within 10 days of the donation.

Later that afternoon, Sean stops by Kirsten's office on his way home.

"Hey there, Kirsten. I wanted to let you know the rumor about County General is true. They are planning on shutting the clinic down the end of next month."

"What are they going to do with the equipment and furnishings?"

"It is still a little early for them to have a formal plan put together. My source said the initial plan is to hold an auction before they close the clinic to get the equipment out of there as soon as possible after the closing."

"How do we get in on the auction, Sean?"

"As soon as I find something out, I will let you know. You may have better luck contacting someone in the finance or administrative offices, though."

"Thanks, Sean, I will get on that first thing tomorrow."

Early the next morning the executive director has the following conversation with Justin Conrad, the director of facilities at County General.

"Justin, if it is okay with you, I would like to put you on the speaker because I have our director of finance, Lauren Gardner, on the call."

"No problem, Kirsten. Hello, Lauren."

"Now that the technology is working, can you tell us, Justin, how County plans on disposing of the equipment at the clinic?"

"We finalized a plan of disposal late last night but there may still be some changes. As of today, the plan is to advertise the sale in the legal notices this Sunday. We will have a walk through for all interested parties to inspect the equipment next Saturday. All bids will need to be sealed and delivered to my office here by 5:00 p.m. three weeks from today. That leaves everyone a week plus to decide what they want and how much it is worth to them. There will be one question and answer session, via teleconference, the Wednesday before the bids are due. This will be the only opportunity interested bidders will have to ask questions about the equipment."

"Justin, will you be issuing formal bid specs or will you post them on your website?"

"Right now the plan is to post them on the website so keep an eye out for them, Kirsten."

"Will do and thanks,Justin. See you a week from Saturday."

Hanging up the phone, Kirsten has the following conversation with Lauren.

"Lauren, I am putting you in charge of this project. I know it is outside your normal assigned duties but Sean and I are too swamped to take care of the details on this. Make sure you put the inspection, conference call Q&A, and the bid due date on all our calendars. Also, check with Sean to see who from our board we can pull in to help with the inspections."

"I want you to monitor County's website at least four times a day until they post the bid specs. As soon as the specs are posted, let me and Sean know. You will be responsible for reviewing the specs and pulling together the final bid. Do you have any questions?"

"I was supposed to go to the satellite office this week and check out some equipment donated by a pediatric group last week. I guess I could put it off or get someone else to take care of it."

"Can you get the receptionist out there to help you with it? You will need to go out there at least once but then have the staff out there make arrangements to ship it here."

"Well, I guess that would work. I will try and get out there tomorrow."

"Thanks, Lauren. I am really counting on you to do some good work on this County General opportunity. Your track record has been somewhat inconsistent lately and I think this will be a great opportunity for you to show me and Sean what you really can do."

"Yeah, thanks Kirsten. I will get to work on things right now."

At the satellite office the next afternoon, Director of Finance Lauren Gardner, meets with the part time receptionist, Candy Walker.

"Wow, look at all this stuff! Do you know what all this stuff does, Candy?"

"Not really, the docs got real excited about it when it was delivered last week, though. I heard one or two of them talking about how valuable it was and that we really should get it to the main clinic as soon as possible."

"Valuable, this stuff? With all these wires and things sticking out, it looks like something we should send to the dump instead of the main clinic. About how much did the doctors think this stuff was worth, Candy?"

"Gee, I think they settled on something like $150,000 in total. They were arguing about it but I remember one doctor saying one particular machine was worth something like $50,000."

"Wow, I had no idea used medical junk could be this valuable. Why did the other doctors want to get rid of it anyway?"

"Beats me, Lauren. What do you want me to do about getting rid of it?"

"Tell you what, Candy. Because it is this valuable, I will take care of it right now. Can you help me get this stuff into my car and I will take it in with me tomorrow morning."

"Works for me, Lauren."

KNOWLEDGE CHECK

2. Which is accurate of Central Clinic's fixed asset policies?

    a. Central Clinic has a fixed asset policy which establishes a capitalization threshold for equipment at $2,500 and for buildings and improvements at $100,000.
    b. In the case of donated equipment, the purchasing clerk is responsible for obtaining information from donors regarding the estimated fair value of donated items.
    c. A large amount of equipment is housed at the satellite clinic location.
    d. Central Clinic uses the same capitalization threshold amount for all classes of capital assets.

The next Saturday, Kirsten, Sean, board member Sal Martin, and his brother-in-law Dean Lewis are at County General inspecting the equipment to be auctioned.

"Thanks for joining us Sal and for bringing your brother -in-law with you."

"Dean, I was so excited to hear you were going to help us outwith this. I can't believe I have the retired director of facilities for County General here with us. It almost seems a bit unfair to the other potential bidders."

"No problem, Kirsten. I'm as excited as you are. It has been a few years since anyone needed my opinion on anything of importance. Please don't tell Mrs. Lewis I said that, however."

An hour later, Kirsten, Sean, Sal, and Dean are having coffee and discussing what they have seen. Dean is finishing his commentary on the condition of the equipment.

"Well, that is what I think. Is this going to be of any help, Sean?"

"It sure is, Dean. I really want to see if we can get the portable MRI machine, the lab equipment we looked at, and two or three of those ultrasound machines. Kirsten, is Lauren ready to get our bid together?"

"She is supposed to be clearing her schedule to be able to work on it full time. Dean, if you don't mind, I would like for you to work directly with Lauren on the amounts and technical specs."

"I would be happy to do it, Kirsten."

"Also, could you explain to me one more time about this grant restriction business you mentioned?"

"Well, like I said earlier, County General purchased a lot of this equipment using grant funds. They are going to need to go back to the various grant agreements and see if they are able to sell the equipment. They may have to transfer some of the grant restrictions to the successful bidder. I had a few minutes to talk with Justin and he said they will have all this figured out by the Q&A teleconference next week.

Probably all you have to worry about is continuing to use any equipment you purchase for the same purpose County General did."

"That doesn't sound like it will be too hard to do. Could you make sure you mention all of this to Lauren?"

"No problem, Kirsten."

Five weeks later, Sean is overseeing the delivery of the equipment they were able to purchase through the County General auction. On one trip to the parking lot, he runs into board member, Sal Martin.

"Hi there, Sal. Did you stop by to watch us get the new equipment installed?"

"To be honest, yes. Dean told me all the equipment you actually bid on and I was anxious to see all of it. Being retired, I do not have much on my calendar these days. I also wanted to see Kirsten for a few minutes but I don't have an appointment and I am not sure if she is in right now."

"Go on in, Sal. She is in today and last I saw she was in her office and the door was open. You better hurry; you never know when she will be on the move again."

Later in Kirsten's office.

"Kirsten, you know I am not one to tell tales but I need to talk to you about something in confidence."

"Let me close my door and then we can talk, Sal. Okay, we have some privacy now."

"I am not one to beat around the bush, Kirsten, so I am going to jump right in here. How well do you know our director of finance?"

"Personally, I don't know her at all other than what I have seen here at the office. As you know, I did not hire her and she probably would not have been my first choice. Her work is marginal and lately her attendance has been erratic. Unfortunately, her work is adequate enough that I can't discipline her. Why do you ask?"

"It is probably nothing, but I am a little suspicious of her and here is why. You know, I am retired and have too much time on my hands. To feel productive, I spend a few hours a week surfing the Net for bargains on anything we might use here at the clinic. Well, yesterday I found several pieces of pediatric equipment on the Internet for a real good price. When I looked up the seller information, I found an interesting seller name."

"Come on Sal, you are killing me here. What was it?"

"Like I said, Kirsten, this may be nothing but I thought 'lauras_secret_garden' looked like it might belong to Lauren. I went into 'Feedback' and this seller, whoever they are, has been selling medical supplies and equipment for the better part of a year. The buyer feedback was pretty good and there were a lot of comments about how quickly the orders had been delivered."

"Thanks for the information, Sal. You know how much I respect and admire you but I need some time to think about this. I have felt that Lauren is not really happy here but, like I said, I don't really know her. I may be getting back with you in a few days to ask some more questions. In the meantime, do you mind keeping tabs on that seller? I would like to know if there is anything for sale that might have been ours at one time."

That afternoon, Sean walks into Kirsten's office with a scowl on his face.

"What is it, Sean? It better not be more bad news, I am already having a bad day."

"Well, I don't know if it's bad news or not. When Sal was here this morning he mentioned something to me about 'all the equipment we bid on' that got me thinking. I was too busy unpacking things at the time to pay it any mind. This afternoon, I was looking at the shipping information and noticed it said sheet one of two. I only have one sheet and it has three of the items where we were the successful bidder. Now, I'm wondering what is on this missing page two."

"Who delivered the equipment to us and when, Sean?"

"I believe it was early this morning before we opened and Lauren was here to sign for it. You really lit a fire under her on this project. I have to say she did a great job of seeing this project through to the end. Kirsten, you look like you just ate a lemon, is anything wrong?"

"Oh dear, I think my day has gone from bad to worse!"

EXERCISES

1. What elements of the fraud triangle are present in this case?

2. What, if any, internal controls are missing or inadequate that might indicate there is a potential for fraud in this case?

3. What controls, if any, could be put in place to minimize the potential for fraud?

4. If you were the executive director in this case, what would you do?

5. Provide some example audit procedures that could help detect this situation.

Chapter 11

Case 11: Procurement Cards

Learning Objectives

After completing this chapter, you should be able to do the following:

- Identify characteristics of effective procurement card policies for a fictitious governmental organization.
- Determine how procurement card policies can be circumvented and lead to fraud in a fictitious governmental organization.

Before We Start

Today a number of state and local governments use procurement cards to streamline the purchasing and payables cycle associated with relatively small, routine, and frequent purchases of operating supplies. Examples of controls over procurement cards that are effective if properly designed and performed include the following:

- Prohibiting the use of procurement cards for the purchase of gift cards.
- Blocking the cash and counter checks options on all procurement cards.
- Having written policies and procedures relating to the issuance and use of procurement cards.
- Requiring employees with procurement cards to execute a cardholder's agreement prior to being issued a procurement card. The agreement should specifically state the
  - employee's responsibilities with respect to the use of the card,
  - consequences if the procurement card is used fraudulently.
- Requiring the submission of receipts for every item on the procurement card statement and a review of the receipts and statement by a responsible and appropriate party.

- Prompt processing of card statements by procurement card holders and timely forward of approved card statements for payment.
- Review of periodic exception reports.
- Random audits of procurement card purchases or statements (or both) by the internal audit or finance or accounting department.

The Case

Leadville is a city in the southwest that uses procurement cards for routine purchases by certain approved individuals. The finance department instituted the "P-Card" program approximately six years ago and it has become very popular among employees and city management.

Originally, the P-Card program was developed to streamline purchasing of day-to-day and routine purchases for all city departments. The P-Card program also eliminated a lot of time spent by accounts payable personnel in processing numerous small or routine purchases from a large number of vendors. Approximately 50 percent of the city's non-personnel expenditures are made using procurement cards.

To compensate for the lack of centralized control, the CFO developed procedures for all personnel involved directly or indirectly in purchasing through the P-Card program. Selected P-Card policy and program controls are as follows:

Leadville **Selected P-Card Policy and Program Controls**
Each department director is allowed to designate which of their staff is to be issued a P-Card. However, only employees at a supervisory level or above are automatically considered eligible for a P-Card.
Employees at less than a supervisory level may be issued a P-Card. In these cases, the department director must prepare a written request stating why the employee needs a P-Card and how he or she will use it. These requests are reviewed and approved by the CFO.
All employees being given P-Card privileges, their immediate supervisor, and their department director sign a P-Card authorization and agreement form. By signing the form, the employee indicates that he or she understands all policies and procedures associated with the P-Card program and that he or she agrees to adhere to them at all times.
Violation of any P-Card policy or procedure may result in the immediate and permanent suspension of an employee's P-Card privileges by the CFO.
P-Card procedures prohibit the use of an employee's P-Card by anyone other than the employee.
When employment is terminated, an employee's P-Card is returned to his or her immediate supervisor.

Leadville Selected P-Card Policy and Program Controls (continued)
Each employee is subject to purchasing limits including maximum daily purchases (number and amount), maximum monthly purchases (number and amount), and maximum per purchase transaction amount. In addition, each employee is limited as to type of merchant based on his or her position, function, and purchasing authority. All dollar and transaction limits, as well as allowable merchant codes, are programmed by the issuing financial institution into the card.
An exception report is electronically transmitted each day to the CFO. The CFO reviews the daily report and sends it to the appropriate department director for review and investigation. Department directors are required to respond to the exception report within five business days.
All purchasing and transaction limits on employees' P-Cards are established by their department director and approved by the CFO. Limits may be increased or decreased at the discretion of the appropriate department director and with approval by the CFO.
Each employee assigned a P-Card is responsible for reconciling his or her monthly statement and attaching the receipts. Employees sign the P-Card statement indicating they have reviewed the purchases and are authorizing them for payment.
An employee's immediate supervisor reviews his or her P-Card statement and all related receipts. The supervisor then approves and signs the monthly P-Card statement and routes it to accounts payable for payment. The supervisor follows up with the employee if any receipts are missing or if any charges appear questionable.
Accounts payable personnel review the P-Card statement for the proper signatures (employee and supervisor) and to determine whether receipts are attached and then input it for payment.
The CFO reserves the right to review any P-Card statement activity at any time.

KNOWLEDGE CHECK

1. Which is accurate of Leadville's P-Card program?

   a. Accounts payable personnel review the P-Card statement but do not look for attached receipts.

   b. Employees sign the P-Card statement indicating they have reviewed the purchases and are authorizing them for payment.

   c. Few employees given P-Card privileges sign a P-Card authorization and agreement form.

   d. Employees assigned a P-Card are not responsible for reconciling their monthly statement and attaching the receipts.

The following occurs outside the office of the public works director, Bob Duncan, early Tuesday morning following Labor Day weekend.

"Hey, Craig. How did you spend the three-day weekend?"

"I had a great time, Bob. Saturday was my brother's birthday so I took the two of us to Vegas to celebrate."

"Wow, three days in Vegas sounds like a lot of fun. How much money did you guys lose?"

"Actually, my brother did okay. As for me, Bob, let's say this trip I made a major contribution to the Nevada economy."

"That bad, huh? Maybe you can make it up on your next trip, but for now it is back to the grind. This morning I need you to run to that little place on Lake Road and get about 50 feet of half inch copper tubing. Last Wednesday I was in the back and noticed our supply was almost gone. We do n't use this size much and I think the last time we got some was three or four months ago. I'm not sure if we still have a valid blanket P.O. with them or not."

"No problem, Bob. I will use my P-Card for the purchase and it should be restocked before lunch."

Later that morning, Craig is at Kraft Supply to pick up the copper tubing.

"Hi there. I'm Craig Sanders with the city and I need to get some copper tubing and a few other things for some jobs we have going."

"Sure thing. What can I get for you?"

"I need 50 feet of half inch for one job, 75 feet of three quarter inch for another job, and then 125 feet of one inch for another job. Because they are different jobs, I need you to ring up each of these separately. Will that be a problem?"

"Nah, that is not a problem. We are happy to be able to help the city."

Craig uses his P-Card to pay for each of the orders and loads the tubing in his city-issued truck.. On his way back to the city storehouse, Craig unloads the three-quarter-inch and one-inch copper tubing at his house. Upon his arrival at the storehouse, he is greeted by his boss, Ricky Hall, the day shift supervisor.

"I appreciate you taking care of this for Bob, Craig. If you had not done it, I would have had to do it and I really did not have time for it this morning. Coming back after a three-day weekend is always tough but we also had two guys call in sick with 'colds' this morning. If you ask me they sounded more like they were suffering from 'too much weekend' instead of colds."

"That is why your job is safe from me, Ricky. The last thing I want to do every day is deal with lying workers and short shifts. You want me to take this copper tubing back and stock it?"

"Yeah, thanks."

Knowledge Check

2. Which is accurate of Leadville's P-Card program?

   a. Employees' immediate supervisors review their P-Card statement and all related receipts.

   b. Supervisors are not responsible for following up with employees if any receipts are missing or if any charges appear questionable.

   c. Employees' immediate supervisors are not required to review their P-Card statements before sending them to accounts payable for payment.

   d. Accounts payable personnel do not review the P-Card statement prior to processing the bill for payment.

Over the next six months, Craig uses his P-Card to purchase various sizes and lengths of copper tubing from Kraft Supply. Each time, he takes the tubing to his house before returning to work. Twice during this time period, his boss sends him to purchase half-inch tubing to restock the city's storehouse.

During spring break Craig takes a few days off for another Vegas vacation. During that time, Ricky Hall sends Keith Stone to Kraft Supply to purchase the little used half-inch copper tubing.

The following conversation takes place between the owner of Kraft Supply and Keith Stone.

"Hi there. I'm Keith Stone with the city and I need to pick up some copper tubing."

"Sure thing. Which size do you need this time and how much?"

"This time? We need what we always get from you the half-inch and 50 feet of it."

While the owner is writing up the order, he says "Where is Craig today?"

"He's taking a few days of R&R in Vegas this week. Apparently, he was not too lucky when he was there last time. Someone said he was going to try and win back some of his losses."

"That sounds like him. Oh, by the way. You make sure to thank your boss for me."

"What do you mean? Thank him for what?"

"You know, all the extra business the city has swung my way this past year. A little shop like mine, we need all the good paying customers we can get."

"Extra business, um, sure thing. I'll tell him."

Upon arriving back at the City storehouse, Keith goes to see Ricky in his office.

"Hey Ricky, do you have a minute?"

"Sure, Keith. What's going on?"

"Well, I don't know if this means anything or not but I just got back with the order of copper tubing you asked me to pick up from Kraft Supply. While I was there, the owner said to thank you for all the extra business this past year. I thought we only used them for this hard to find half-inch that we only use a few times a year?"

"As far as I know that is all we get from him. Maybe he got us confused with the county."

"Could be. He knew Craig by name which I thought was a little strange. It almost sounded like he knew him a little, too. He even laughed and joked about him when I sai d Craig was off in Vegas this week."

"Well, I have sent Craig there a few times this year to get the half inch. Maybe he got to know Craig that way. Hey, if you still feel funny about it, why not call that city hotline they have for employees and report it?"

"I may do that, Ricky. Thanks for listening. I am probably reading far more into this than there is."

Later that week, Keith does call the city's Fraud, Waste, and Abuse Hotline. A subsequent investigation found Craig purchased more than $45,000 of copper tubing using his P-Card over a nine-month period.

KNOWLEDGE CHECK

3. Which is accurate of Leadville's P-Card program?

   a. The CFO reserves the right to review any P-Card statement activity at any time.
   b. An exception report is electronically transmitted each day to the individual P-Card holder.
   c. All dollar and transaction limits, as well as allowable merchant codes, are programmed by accounts payable into the card.
   d. The P-Card authorization and agreement form is signed by only the employee being given P-Card privileges.

EXERCISES

1. Aside from the fraud that occurred in this case, do you think the city's P-Card policies and procedures were adequate? Why or why not?

2. What are some controls you would add to the P-Card program?

3. Why did this situation go undetected for almost a year? What could the public works department have done to prevent and detect this type of fraud?

4. What are some audit procedures that could be used to test controls and activity related to procurement cards?

Chapter 12

Case 12: Overtime Fraud

Learning Objectives

- Identify how personnel policies and procedures in a fictitious government can be circumvented and lead to possible fraud or abuse.
- Determine the importance of understanding the environment in which a fictitious government entity operates and how it may affect the development and execution of personnel policies and procedures.

Before We Start

In many not-for-profit (NFP) entities, salaries and benefits represent the major natural expense category. Employees of NFPs are often paid less than their counterparts in the private sector which may lead some employees to rationalize misappropriation of assets as compensation for their low salary levels. Additionally, work force reductions or reduced hours in times of limited resources may create an unstable work environment. These circumstances may pressure employees to work a second job while "on the clock" of their NFP employer. Low pay, reduced hours, and increased work load often create incentives for employees to misappropriate assets by recording time not actually worked for the benefit of their NFP employer.

Payroll and personnel controls, and therefore audit procedures, typically focus on the accuracy of the amounts paid (paid for actual hours worked at an approved rate of pay) as indicated on the manual or electronic time records and documented in an employee's personnel file. In some NFPs employees may not work a standard 40-hour 8 a.m. to 5 p.m. work week.

Controls relating to time worked do not often focus on the legitimacy of hours worked outside the regular work day or work week. In NFPs, the approval of an employee's supervisor may be the only evidence that the time worked is legitimate. Unfortunately, the supervisor may not be personally aware of whether the employee actually worked the hours indicated on the time record.

THE CASE

Helping Hands is a 501(c)(3) organization whose mission is to provide transportation services between home and work, at no cost, to developmentally disabled adults. The service area encompasses the three counties comprising the metropolitan statistical area (MSA). Clients are transported from home to work and back in 14-passenger vans driven by qualified individuals with a current commercial driver's license (CDL) and accompanied by a transportation assistant.

Helping Hands receives funding from the state Department of Transportation (DOT) as well as from the state Department of Health and Human Services (HHS). Additional funds are obtained through an annual fund raising campaign, a twice-yearly fund raising dinner, and an endowment established at the local community foundation.

The organization has been in existence five years and has a high demand for its services. Even though the unemployment rate in the MSA is high, individuals with a CDL are in high demand, Helping Hands is often understaffed. The six weeks needed to process an applicant's application and conduct the necessary health screening and background investigation often exacerbate the understaffed situation. In some cases, volunteers that have been previously screened and investigated are used to fill in when the organization is understaffed. In the past two years, Helping Hands has incurred a significant amount of overtime due to the understaffed situation.

Due to a five-year mandatory auditor rotation policy, a new audit firm was recently selected to replace the former firm which provided audit services to Helping Hands during its first five years of operations. During the preliminary planning for the engagement, the in-charge auditor, Beth Marks reviews the Payroll Procedures Manual and notes the following:

Helping Hands **Payroll Procedures Manual Excerpts**
All employees are paid every other Friday based on the time worked in the previous full two-week period.
All employees (exempt and hourly) complete a bi-weekly time sheet. For hourly employees, a time card supports the time worked on the time sheet. By signing the time sheet, employees indicate the total and type of hours worked are true and correct.
Employees working for more than one program, division, or department allocate the total time spent to each program, division, and department on the face of their time sheets.
An employee's immediate supervisor signs his or her time sheet indicating approval of the regular and overtime hours worked.
Overtime is to be kept to a minimum and only incurred when it is necessary to provide services to Helping Hands clients. All overtime is to be approved by an employee's immediate supervisor.
Departments and divisions within Helping Hands submit complete and signed time cards to the payroll department by noon every other Monday.
Payroll department personnel verify the math accuracy of each time sheet and ascertain it has been signed by the employee and his or her supervisor. The payroll clerk enters the information from the time sheet into the payroll system for processing.

Knowledge Check

1. Which is NOT accurate of Helping Hands?

   a. The unemployment rate is low and individuals with a CDL are in low demand.
   b. Helping Hands' mission is to provide transportation services between home and work, at no cost, to developmentally disabled adults.
   c. The service area encompasses the three counties that make up the metropolitan area.
   d. Helping Hands has been in existence for over 25 years.

As part of the preliminary audit planning, Beth Marks obtains interim financial statements from the CFO for Helping Hands, Jeff Carter. She also obtains the year-to-date program budget reports. From this information, Beth concludes, among other things, payroll is a significant expense (that is, 65 percent of total expenses) for Helping Hands.

At the engagement brainstorming session, payroll is identified as a potential fraud risk and a number of preliminary audit procedures are identified as being necessary.

The following conversation takes place between the engagement in-charge, Beth Marks, and Jeff Carter, the CFO.

"Jeff, I am not sure how much time your former auditors spent with you discussing potential areas where fraud might occur. My firm makes it a standard audit procedure to talk to an organization's CFO about where they think fraud might occur in their organization. Where do you think you might be subject to fraud here at Helping Hands?"

"I am glad you asked me this, Beth, because our former auditors talked only to the CEO about these types of things. I think one of the areas we may be at risk for fraud is in our procurement of van maintenance and related supplies. No one around here knows what most of the things are that the garage supervisor, George Stone, buys. We all kind of take his word on things."

"This is a good area for us to review. What would you say is your biggest line item expense?"

"That is a no-brainer, Beth. Payroll is our biggest expense and because of that we have what I think are some pretty strong controls in place."

"Do you think you are at risk for any payroll fraud, Jeff?"

"I don't really think we are. Our hiring process is pretty tight what with the background and CDL checks. These make me pretty sure we are not at risk for any fictitious employees."

"Looking at those financial statements you gave me I could not help but notice there is a significant amount of overtime in this organization. From what I could tell, most of the overtime is incurred in the garage and transportation programs. Why is that?"

"You know what the labor supply is around here right now. The tight labor market for these types of positions makes it difficult for us to hire and keep transportation assistants and garage staff. A good mechanic is hard to find and extremely expensive when you do find one. We have been operating mostly with George and his number one mechanic, Stan, most of the last year. The two of them are working a lot of evenings and weekends to keep the fleet on the streets."

"What is causing the overtime in the transportation program? Because you are using qualified volunteers as transportation assistants, I would not think you would have a lot of overtime in this program."

"It's not the transportation assistants, Beth. We have a huge problem finding and keeping drivers. The demand right now for CDLs is fierce. With what we pay, it has been difficult getting licensed drivers to come and work for us. Can you blame somebody for leaving our $20 an hour job for one that pays them $30 an hour? We have even talked about hiring promising individuals and paying for them to get their CDL. For the past six months, four of our drivers have been working 14 hour days because we have been short two drivers."

"Does someone approve all of the overtime before it is worked?"

"Not really. Walt Breen, our transportation supervisor, signs off on their time sheets as to hours worked but I am not sure what they have in place as approval for overtime in advance."

"Thanks Jeff. Could you set me up to see George and Walt later today? I would like to get some more information from them."

KNOWLEDGE CHECK

2. Which is accurate of Helping Hands payroll procedures?

   a. The payroll clerk enters the information from the time sheet into the payroll system for processing.
   b. Payroll department personnel do not ascertain that time sheets have been signed by the employee.
   c. Payroll department personnel do not ascertain that time sheets have been signed by the employee's supervisor.
   d. All overtime is approved by an employee's supervisor before it is worked.

Later, at the meeting with in-charge Beth Marks, Garage Supervisor George Stone, and Transportation Supervisor Walt Breen.

"Okay, gentlemen, I think I got all of my questions answered. Basically, overtime is not approved in advance because everyone off-site and in the office knows how short-staffed you are. To compensate for this, you approve overtime in arrears when you sign off on the employee time cards. Does that about sum it up?"

Walt looks at George and says "By George, I think she's got it."

After discussing her findings with the engagement partner, it is determined that payroll, and specifically, overtime is a fraud risk area. Beth develops additional audit procedures related to payroll and overtime. Later that week, the staff auditor assigned to the engagement, Jonathon Bullock, asks Beth to come and look over the results of his payroll test work.

"Beth, I am not sure what any of this means but I wanted to bring it to your attention. Look at these timesheets for these four drivers. They are for different pay periods but each of them has the same amount of regular and overtime hours. This driver here has a route that is within two miles of the garage and this driver has a route that goes all the way out to the west side of the city and back. It doesn't make sense that they would both have the same amount of overtime. Not only that, but this first driver appears to forget to clock out two to three times each week. The third time sheet is really confusing to me because it has overtime hours for a Saturday. The clients usually work Monday through Friday, right?"

KNOWLEDGE CHECK

3. Which is accurate of Helping Hands' payroll procedures?

    a. Payroll personnel do not verify the math accuracy of each time sheet.
    b. All overtime is to be approved by an employee's immediate supervisor.
    c. Overtime is encouraged.
    d. Only overtime incurred on weekends is required to be approved in advance by an employee's supervisor.

"That is true, Jonathon. Normal work days are Monday through Friday. But look closer, the time sheet was approved by George, who is the garage supervisor. Walt Breen is supposed to sign the drivers' time sheets. What is the issue with the time sheet for the fourth driver?"

"I hope you don't think I'm crazy, but the fourth time sheet is too clean. See how most of the others are smudged or have the corners frayed? Now look at this one. What do you think, Beth?"

EXERCISES

1. How would you resolve the issues presented in this case?

2. Would you consider these situations fraudulent or indicative of abuse?

Appendix A

AU-C SECTION 240

AU-C Section 240 *

Consideration of Fraud in a Financial Statement Audit

Source: SAS No. 122.

Effective for audits of financial statements for periods ending on or after December 15, 2012.

Introduction

Scope of This Section

.01 This section addresses the auditor's responsibilities relating to fraud in an audit of financial statements. Specifically, it expands on how section 315, *Understanding the Entity and Its Environment and Assessing the Risks of Material Misstatement*, and section 330, *Performing Audit Procedures in Response to Assessed Risks and Evaluating the Audit Evidence Obtained*, are to be applied regarding risks of material misstatement due to fraud.

Characteristics of Fraud

.02 Misstatements in the financial statements can arise from either fraud or error. The distinguishing factor between fraud and error is whether the underlying action that results in the misstatement of the financial statements is intentional or unintentional.

.03 Although fraud is a broad legal concept, for the purposes of generally accepted auditing standards (GAAS), the auditor is primarily concerned with fraud that causes a material misstatement in the financial statements. Two types of intentional misstatements are relevant to the auditor—misstatements resulting from fraudulent financial reporting and misstatements resulting from misappropriation of assets. Although the auditor may suspect or, in rare cases, identify the occurrence of fraud, the auditor does not make legal determinations of whether fraud has actually occurred. (Ref: par. .A1–.A8)

Responsibility for the Prevention and Detection of Fraud

.04 The primary responsibility for the prevention and detection of fraud rests with both those charged with governance of the entity and management. It is important that management, with the oversight of those charged with governance, places a strong emphasis on fraud prevention, which may reduce opportunities for fraud to take place, and fraud deterrence, which could persuade individuals not to commit fraud because of the likelihood of detection and punishment. This involves a commitment to creating a culture of honesty and ethical behavior, which can be reinforced by active oversight by those

---

* This section contains an "AU-C" identifier instead of an "AU" identifier. "AU-C" is a temporary identifier to avoid confusion with references to existing "AU" sections, which remain effective through 2013. The "AU-C" identifier will revert to "AU" in 2014, by which time this section becomes fully effective for all engagements.

charged with governance. Oversight by those charged with governance includes considering the potential for override of controls or other inappropriate influence over the financial reporting process, such as efforts by management to manage earnings in order to influence the perceptions of financial statement users regarding the entity's performance and profitability.

Responsibilities of the Auditor

.05 An auditor conducting an audit in accordance with GAAS is responsible for obtaining reasonable assurance that the financial statements as a whole are free from material misstatement, whether caused by fraud or error. Due to the inherent limitations of an audit, an unavoidable risk exists that some material misstatements of the financial statements may not be detected, even though the audit is properly planned and performed in accordance with GAAS.[1]

.06 As described in section 200, *Overall Objectives of the Independent Auditor and the Conduct of an Audit in Accordance With Generally Accepted Auditing Standards*, the potential effects of inherent limitations are particularly significant in the case of misstatement resulting from fraud.[2] The risk of not detecting a material misstatement resulting from fraud is higher than the risk of not detecting one resulting from error. This is because fraud may involve sophisticated and carefully organized schemes designed to conceal it, such as forgery, deliberate failure to record transactions, or intentional misrepresentations being made to the auditor. Such attempts at concealment may be even more difficult to detect when accompanied by collusion. Collusion may cause the auditor to believe that audit evidence is persuasive when it is, in fact, false. The auditor's ability to detect a fraud depends on factors such as the skillfulness of the perpetrator, the frequency and extent of manipulation, the degree of collusion involved, the relative size of individual amounts manipulated, and the seniority of those individuals involved. Although the auditor may be able to identify potential opportunities for fraud to be perpetrated, it is difficult for the auditor to determine whether misstatements in judgment areas, such as accounting estimates, are caused by fraud or error.

.07 Furthermore, the risk of the auditor not detecting a material misstatement resulting from management fraud is greater than for employee fraud because management is frequently in a position to directly or indirectly manipulate accounting records, present fraudulent financial information, or override control procedures designed to prevent similar frauds by other employees.

.08 When obtaining reasonable assurance, the auditor is responsible for maintaining professional skepticism throughout the audit, considering the potential for management override of controls, and recognizing the fact that audit procedures that are effective for detecting error may not be effective in detecting fraud. The requirements in this section are designed to assist the auditor in identifying and assessing the risks of material misstatement due to fraud and in designing procedures to detect such misstatement.

Effective Date

.09 This section is effective for audits of financial statements for periods ending on or after December 15, 2012.

---

[1] Paragraphs .A55–.A56 of section 200, *Overall Objectives of the Independent Auditor and the Conduct of an Audit in Accordance With Generally Accepted Auditing Standards*.

[2] Paragraph .A55 of section 200.

Objectives

.10 The objectives of the auditor are to

a. identify and assess the risks of material misstatement of the financial statements due to fraud;

b. obtain sufficient appropriate audit evidence regarding the assessed risks of material misstatement due to fraud, through designing and implementing appropriate responses; and

c. respond appropriately to fraud or suspected fraud identified during the audit.

Definitions

.11 For purposes of GAAS, the following terms have the meanings attributed as follows:

Fraud. An intentional act by one or more individuals among management, those charged with governance, employees, or third parties, involving the use of deception that results in a misstatement in financial statements that are the subject of an audit.

Fraud risk factors. Events or conditions that indicate an incentive or pressure to perpetrate fraud, provide an opportunity to commit fraud, or indicate attitudes or rationalizations to justify a fraudulent action. (Ref: par. .A11, .A30, and .A56)

Requirements

Professional Skepticism

.12 In accordance with section 200, the auditor should maintain professional skepticism throughout the audit, recognizing the possibility that a material misstatement due to fraud could exist, notwithstanding the auditor's past experience of the honesty and integrity of the entity's management and those charged with governance.[3] (Ref: par. .A9–.A10)

.13 Unless the auditor has reason to believe the contrary, the auditor may accept records and documents as genuine. If conditions identified during the audit cause the auditor to believe that a document may not be authentic or that terms in a document have been modified but not disclosed to the auditor, the auditor should investigate further. (Ref: par. .A11)

.14 When responses to inquiries of management, those charged with governance, or others are inconsistent or otherwise unsatisfactory (for example, vague or implausible), the auditor should further investigate the inconsistencies or unsatisfactory responses.

Discussion Among the Engagement Team

.15 Section 315 requires a discussion among the key engagement team members, including the engagement partner, and a determination by the engagement partner of which matters are to be communicated to those team

---

[3] Paragraph .17 of section 200.

members not involved in the discussion.[4] This discussion should include an exchange of ideas or brainstorming among the engagement team members about how and where the entity's financial statements might be susceptible to material misstatement due to fraud, how management could perpetrate and conceal fraudulent financial reporting, and how assets of the entity could be misappropriated. The discussion should occur setting aside beliefs that the engagement team members may have that management and those charged with governance are honest and have integrity, and should, in particular, also address (Ref: par. .A12–.A13)

- *a.* known external and internal factors affecting the entity that may create an incentive or pressure for management or others to commit fraud, provide the opportunity for fraud to be perpetrated, and indicate a culture or environment that enables management or others to rationalize committing fraud;
- *b.* the risk of management override of controls;
- *c.* consideration of circumstances that might be indicative of earnings management or manipulation of other financial measures and the practices that might be followed by management to manage earnings or other financial measures that could lead to fraudulent financial reporting;
- *d.* the importance of maintaining professional skepticism throughout the audit regarding the potential for material misstatement due to fraud; and
- *e.* how the auditor might respond to the susceptibility of the entity's financial statements to material misstatement due to fraud.

Communication among the engagement team members about the risks of material misstatement due to fraud should continue throughout the audit, particularly upon discovery of new facts during the audit.

Risk Assessment Procedures and Related Activities

.16 When performing risk assessment procedures and related activities to obtain an understanding of the entity and its environment, including the entity's internal control, required by section 315, the auditor should perform the procedures in paragraphs .17–.24 to obtain information for use in identifying the risks of material misstatement due to fraud.[5]

Discussions With Management and Others Within the Entity

.17 The auditor should make inquiries of management regarding

- *a.* management's assessment of the risk that the financial statements may be materially misstated due to fraud, including the nature, extent, and frequency of such assessments; (Ref: par. .A14–.A15)
- *b.* management's process for identifying, responding to, and monitoring the risks of fraud in the entity, including any specific risks of fraud that management has identified or that have been brought to its attention, or classes of transactions, account balances, or disclosures for which a risk of fraud is likely to exist; (Ref: par. .A16)

---

[4] Paragraph .11 of section 315, *Understanding the Entity and Its Environment and Assessing the Risks of Material Misstatement*.

[5] Paragraphs .05–.25 of section 315.

c. management's communication, if any, to those charged with governance regarding its processes for identifying and responding to the risks of fraud in the entity; and

d. management's communication, if any, to employees regarding its views on business practices and ethical behavior.

.18 The auditor should make inquiries of management, and others within the entity as appropriate, to determine whether they have knowledge of any actual, suspected, or alleged fraud affecting the entity. (Ref: par. .A17–.A20)

.19 For those entities that have an internal audit function,[6] the auditor should make inquiries of internal audit to obtain its views about the risks of fraud; determine whether it has knowledge of any actual, suspected, or alleged fraud affecting the entity; whether it has performed any procedures to identify or detect fraud during the year; and whether management has satisfactorily responded to any findings resulting from these procedures.

Those Charged With Governance

.20 Unless all of those charged with governance are involved in managing the entity,[7] the auditor should obtain an understanding of how those charged with governance exercise oversight of management's processes for identifying and responding to the risks of fraud in the entity and the internal control that management has established to mitigate these risks. (Ref: par. .A21–.A23)

.21 Unless all of those charged with governance are involved in managing the entity, the auditor should make inquiries of those charged with governance (or the audit committee or, at least, its chair) to determine their views about the risks of fraud and whether they have knowledge of any actual, suspected, or alleged fraud affecting the entity. These inquiries are made, in part, to corroborate the responses received from the inquiries of management.

Unusual or Unexpected Relationships Identified

.22 Based on analytical procedures performed as part of risk assessment procedures,[8] the auditor should evaluate whether unusual or unexpected relationships that have been identified indicate risks of material misstatement due to fraud. To the extent not already included, the analytical procedures, and evaluation thereof, should include procedures relating to revenue accounts. (Ref: par. .A24–.A26 and .A46)

Other Information

.23 The auditor should consider whether other information obtained by the auditor indicates risks of material misstatement due to fraud. (Ref: par. .A27)

---

[6] Section 610, *The Auditor's Consideration of the Internal Audit Function in an Audit of Financial Statements* , provides guidance in audits of those entities that have an internal audit function. Statement on Auditing Standards (SAS) No. 65, *The Auditor's Consideration of the Internal Audit Function in an Audit of Financial Statements,* is currently effective and codified as AU section 322. SAS No. 65 has been included in section 610, as designated by SAS No. 122, *Statements on Auditing Standards: Clarification and Recodification,* and will be superseded when it is redrafted for clarity and convergence with International Standard on Auditing 610 (Revised), *Using the Work of Internal Auditors,* as part of the Clarification and Convergence project of the Auditing Standards Board. Until such time, section 610 has been conformed to reflect updated section and paragraph cross references but has not otherwise been subjected to a comprehensive review or revision.

[7] Paragraph .09 of section 260, *The Auditor's Communication With Those Charged With Governance.*

[8] Paragraphs .06(*b*) and .A7–.A10 of section 315.

Evaluation of Fraud Risk Factors

.24 The auditor should evaluate whether the information obtained from the risk assessment procedures and related activities performed indicates that one or more fraud risk factors are present. Although fraud risk factors may not necessarily indicate the existence of fraud, they have often been present in circumstances in which frauds have occurred and, therefore, may indicate risks of material misstatement due to fraud. (Ref: par. .A28–.A32)

Identification and Assessment of the Risks of Material Misstatement Due to Fraud

.25 In accordance with section 315, the auditor should identify and assess the risks of material misstatement due to fraud at the financial statement level, and at the assertion level for classes of transactions, account balances, and disclosures.[9] The auditor's risk assessment should be ongoing throughout the audit, following the initial assessment.

.26 When identifying and assessing the risks of material misstatement due to fraud, the auditor should, based on a presumption that risks of fraud exist in revenue recognition, evaluate which types of revenue, revenue transactions, or assertions give rise to such risks. Paragraph .46 specifies the documentation required when the auditor concludes that the presumption is not applicable in the circumstances of the engagement and, accordingly, has not identified revenue recognition as a risk of material misstatement due to fraud. (Ref: par. .A33–.A35)

.27 The auditor should treat those assessed risks of material misstatement due to fraud as significant risks and, accordingly, to the extent not already done so, the auditor should obtain an understanding of the entity's related controls, including control activities, relevant to such risks, including the evaluation of whether such controls have been suitably designed and implemented to mitigate such fraud risks. (Ref: par. .A36–.A37)

Responses to the Assessed Risks of Material Misstatement Due to Fraud

Overall Responses

.28 In accordance with section 330, the auditor should determine overall responses to address the assessed risks of material misstatement due to fraud at the financial statement level.[10] (Ref: par. .A38)

.29 In determining overall responses to address the assessed risks of material misstatement due to fraud at the financial statement level, the auditor should

a. assign and supervise personnel, taking into account the knowledge, skill, and ability of the individuals to be given significant engagement responsibilities and the auditor's assessment of the risks of material misstatement due to fraud for the engagement; (Ref: par. .A39–.A40)

---

[9] Paragraph .26 of section 315.

[10] Paragraph .05 of section 330, *Performing Audit Procedures in Response to Assessed Risks and Evaluating the Audit Evidence Obtained.*

b. evaluate whether the selection and application of accounting policies by the entity, particularly those related to subjective measurements and complex transactions, may be indicative of fraudulent financial reporting resulting from management's effort to manage earnings, or a bias that may create a material misstatement; and (Ref: par. .A41)

c. incorporate an element of unpredictability in the selection of the nature, timing, and extent of audit procedures. (Ref: par. .A42)

Audit Procedures Responsive to Assessed Risks of Material Misstatement Due to Fraud at the Assertion Level

.30 In accordance with section 330, the auditor should design and perform further audit procedures whose nature, timing, and extent are responsive to the assessed risks of material misstatement due to fraud at the assertion level.[11] (Ref: par. .A43–.A46)

Audit Procedures Responsive to Risks Related to Management Override of Controls

.31 Management is in a unique position to perpetrate fraud because of management's ability to manipulate accounting records and prepare fraudulent financial statements by overriding controls that otherwise appear to be operating effectively. Although the level of risk of management override of controls will vary from entity to entity, the risk is, nevertheless, present in all entities. Due to the unpredictable way in which such override could occur, it is a risk of material misstatement due to fraud and, thus, a significant risk.

.32 Even if specific risks of material misstatement due to fraud are not identified by the auditor, a possibility exists that management override of controls could occur. Accordingly, the auditor should address the risk of management override of controls apart from any conclusions regarding the existence of more specifically identifiable risks by designing and performing audit procedures to

a. test the appropriateness of journal entries recorded in the general ledger and other adjustments made in the preparation of the financial statements, including entries posted directly to financial statement drafts. In designing and performing audit procedures for such tests, the auditor should (Ref: par. .A47–.A50 and .A55)

i. obtain an understanding of the entity's financial reporting process and controls over journal entries and other adjustments,[12] and the suitability of design and implementation of such controls;

ii. make inquiries of individuals involved in the financial reporting process about inappropriate or unusual activity relating to the processing of journal entries and other adjustments;

iii. consider fraud risk indicators, the nature and complexity of accounts, and entries processed outside the normal course of business;

iv. select journal entries and other adjustments made at the end of a reporting period; and

---

[11] Paragraph .06 of section 330.

[12] Paragraph .19 of section 315.

v. consider the need to test journal entries and other adjustments throughout the period.

b. review accounting estimates for biases and evaluate whether the circumstances producing the bias, if any, represent a risk of material misstatement due to fraud. In performing this review, the auditor should

i. evaluate whether the judgments and decisions made by management in making the accounting estimates included in the financial statements, even if they are individually reasonable, indicate a possible bias on the part of the entity's management that may represent a risk of material misstatement due to fraud. If so, the auditor should reevaluate the accounting estimates taken as a whole, and

ii. perform a retrospective review of management judgments and assumptions related to significant accounting estimates reflected in the financial statements of the prior year. Estimates selected for review should include those that are based on highly sensitive assumptions or are otherwise significantly affected by judgments made by management. (Ref: par. .A51–.A53)

c. evaluate, for significant transactions that are outside the normal course of business for the entity or that otherwise appear to be unusual given the auditor's understanding of the entity and its environment and other information obtained during the audit, whether the business rationale (or the lack thereof) of the transactions suggests that they may have been entered into to engage in fraudulent financial reporting or to conceal misappropriation of assets. (Ref: par. .A54)

Other Audit Procedures

.33 The auditor should determine whether, in order to respond to the identified risks of management override of controls, the auditor needs to perform other audit procedures in addition to those specifically referred to previously (that is, when specific additional risks of management override exist that are not covered as part of the procedures performed to address the requirements in paragraph .32). (Ref: par. .A55)

Evaluation of Audit Evidence (Ref: par. .A56)

.34 The auditor should evaluate, at or near the end of the audit, whether the accumulated results of auditing procedures (including analytical procedures that were performed as substantive tests or when forming an overall conclusion) affect the assessment of the risks of material misstatement due to fraud made earlier in the audit or indicate a previously unrecognized risk of material misstatement due to fraud. If not already performed when forming an overall conclusion, the analytical procedures relating to revenue, required by paragraph .22, should be performed through the end of the reporting period. (Ref: par. .A57–.A58)

.35 If the auditor identifies a misstatement, the auditor should evaluate whether such a misstatement is indicative of fraud. If such an indication exists, the auditor should evaluate the implications of the misstatement with regard to other aspects of the audit, particularly the auditor's evaluation of materiality, management and employee integrity, and the reliability of management representations, recognizing that an instance of fraud is unlikely to be an isolated occurrence. (Ref: par. .A59–.A62)

.36 If the auditor identifies a misstatement, whether material or not, and the auditor has reason to believe that it is, or may be, the result of fraud and that management (in particular, senior management) is involved, the auditor should reevaluate the assessment of the risks of material misstatement due to fraud and its resulting effect on the nature, timing, and extent of audit procedures to respond to the assessed risks. The auditor should also consider whether circumstances or conditions indicate possible collusion involving employees, management, or third parties when reconsidering the reliability of evidence previously obtained. (Ref: par. .A60)

.37 If the auditor concludes that, or is unable to conclude whether, the financial statements are materially misstated as a result of fraud, the auditor should evaluate the implications for the audit. (Ref: par. .A61)

Auditor Unable to Continue the Engagement

.38 If, as a result of identified fraud or suspected fraud, the auditor encounters circumstances that bring into question the auditor's ability to continue performing the audit, the auditor should

a. determine the professional and legal responsibilities applicable in the circumstances, including whether a requirement exists for the auditor to report to the person or persons who engaged the auditor or, in some cases, to regulatory authorities;

b. consider whether it is appropriate to withdraw from the engagement, when withdrawal is possible under applicable law or regulation; and

c. if the auditor withdraws

   i. discuss with the appropriate level of management and those charged with governance the auditor's withdrawal from the engagement and the reasons for the withdrawal, and

   ii. determine whether a professional or legal requirement exists to report to the person or persons who engaged the auditor or, in some cases, to regulatory authorities, the auditor's withdrawal from the engagement and the reasons for the withdrawal. (Ref: par. .A63–.A66)

Communications to Management and With Those Charged With Governance

.39 If the auditor has identified a fraud or has obtained information that indicates that a fraud may exist, the auditor should communicate these matters on a timely basis to the appropriate level of management in order to inform those with primary responsibility for the prevention and detection of fraud of matters relevant to their responsibilities. (Ref: par. .A67)

.40 Unless all of those charged with governance are involved in managing the entity, if the auditor has identified or suspects fraud involving

a. management,

b. employees who have significant roles in internal control, or

c. others, when the fraud results in a material misstatement in the financial statements, the auditor should communicate these matters to those charged with governance on a timely basis. If the auditor suspects fraud involving management, the auditor should communicate these suspicions to those charged with governance and discuss with them the nature, timing, and extent of audit procedures necessary to complete the audit. (Ref: par. .A68–.A70)

.41 The auditor should communicate with those charged with governance any other matters related to fraud that are, in the auditor's professional judgment, relevant to their responsibilities. (Ref: par. .A71)

Communications to Regulatory and Enforcement Authorities

.42 If the auditor has identified or suspects a fraud, the auditor should determine whether the auditor has a responsibility to report the occurrence or suspicion to a party outside the entity. Although the auditor's professional duty to maintain the confidentiality of client information may preclude such reporting, the auditor's legal responsibilities may override the duty of confidentiality in some circumstances. (Ref: par. .A72–.A74)

Documentation

.43 The auditor should include in the audit documentation[13] of the auditor's understanding of the entity and its environment and the assessment of the risks of material misstatement required by section 315 the following:[14]

a. The significant decisions reached during the discussion among the engagement team regarding the susceptibility of the entity's financial statements to material misstatement due to fraud, and how and when the discussion occurred and the audit team members who participated

b. The identified and assessed risks of material misstatement due to fraud at the financial statement level and at the assertion level (See paragraphs .16–.27.)

.44 The auditor should include in the audit documentation of the auditor's responses to the assessed risks of material misstatement required by section 330 the following:[15]

a. The overall responses to the assessed risks of material misstatement due to fraud at the financial statement level and the nature, timing, and extent of audit procedures, and the linkage of those procedures with the assessed risks of material misstatement due to fraud at the assertion level

b. The results of the audit procedures, including those designed to address the risk of management override of controls

.45 The auditor should include in the audit documentation communications about fraud made to management, those charged with governance, regulators, and others.

.46 If the auditor has concluded that the presumption that there is a risk of material misstatement due to fraud related to revenue recognition is overcome in the circumstances of the engagement, the auditor should include in the audit documentation the reasons for that conclusion.

---

[13] Paragraphs .08–.12 and .A8 of section 230, *Audit Documentation*.

[14] Paragraph .33 of section 315.

[15] Paragraph .30 of section 330.

Application and Other Explanatory Material

Characteristics of Fraud (Ref: par. .03)

.A1 Fraud, whether fraudulent financial reporting or misappropriation of assets, involves incentive or pressure to commit fraud, a perceived opportunity to do so, and some rationalization of the act, as follows:

- Incentive or pressure to commit fraudulent financial reporting may exist when management is under pressure, from sources outside or inside the entity, to achieve an expected (and perhaps, unrealistic) earnings target or financial outcome—particularly because the consequences to management for failing to meet financial goals can be significant. Similarly, individuals may have an incentive to misappropriate assets (for example, because the individuals are living beyond their means).
- A perceived opportunity to commit fraud may exist when an individual believes internal control can be overridden (for example, because the individual is in a position of trust or has knowledge of specific deficiencies in internal control).
- Individuals may be able to rationalize committing a fraudulent act. Some individuals possess an attitude, character, or set of ethical values that allow them knowingly and intentionally to commit a dishonest act. However, even otherwise honest individuals can commit fraud in an environment that imposes sufficient pressure on them.

.A2 Fraudulent financial reporting involves intentional misstatements, including omissions of amounts or disclosures in financial statements to deceive financial statement users. It can be caused by the efforts of management to manage earnings in order to deceive financial statement users by influencing their perceptions about the entity's performance and profitability. Such earnings management may start out with small actions or inappropriate adjustment of assumptions and changes in judgments by management. Pressures and incentives may lead these actions to increase to the extent that they result in fraudulent financial reporting. Such a situation could occur when, due to pressures to meet expectations or a desire to maximize compensation based on performance, management intentionally takes positions that lead to fraudulent financial reporting by materially misstating the financial statements. In some entities, management may be motivated to reduce earnings by a material amount to minimize tax or to inflate earnings to secure bank financing.

.A3 An auditor conducting an audit in accordance with GAAS is responsible for obtaining reasonable assurance about whether the financial statements as a whole are free from material misstatement, whether caused by fraud or error. Accordingly, the auditor is primarily concerned with fraud that causes a material misstatement of the financial statements. However, in conducting the audit, the auditor may identify misstatements arising from fraud that are not material to the financial statements. Paragraphs .35–.36 and .39–.42 address the auditor's responsibilities in such circumstances in evaluating audit evidence and in communicating audit findings, respectively.

.A4 Intent is often difficult to determine, particularly in matters involving accounting estimates and the application of accounting principles. For example, unreasonable accounting estimates may be unintentional or may be the result of an intentional attempt to misstate the financial statements. Although an audit is not designed to determine intent, the auditor's objective is to obtain reasonable assurance about whether the financial statements as a whole are free from material misstatement, whether due to fraud or error.[16]

.A5 Fraudulent financial reporting may be accomplished by the following:

- Manipulation, falsification (including forgery), or alteration of accounting records or supporting documentation from which the financial statements are prepared
- Misrepresentation in, or intentional omission from, the financial statements of events, transactions, or other significant information
- Intentional misapplication of accounting principles relating to amounts, classification, manner of presentation, or disclosure

.A6 Fraudulent financial reporting often involves management override of controls that otherwise may appear to be operating effectively. Fraud can be committed by management overriding controls using such techniques as the following:

- Recording fictitious journal entries, particularly close to the end of an accounting period, to manipulate operating results or achieve other objectives
- Inappropriately adjusting assumptions and changing judgments used to estimate account balances
- Omitting, advancing, or delaying recognition in the financial statements of events and transactions that have occurred during the reporting period
- Concealing, or not disclosing, facts that could affect the amounts recorded in the financial statements
- Engaging in complex transactions that are structured to misrepresent the financial position or financial performance of the entity
- Altering records and terms related to significant and unusual transactions

.A7 Misappropriation of assets involves the theft of an entity's assets and is often perpetrated by employees in relatively small and immaterial amounts. However, it can also involve management, who is usually better able to disguise or conceal misappropriations in ways that are difficult to detect. Misappropriation of assets can be accomplished in a variety of ways including the following:

- Embezzling receipts (for example, misappropriating collections on accounts receivable or diverting receipts from written-off accounts to personal bank accounts)
- Stealing physical assets or intellectual property (for example, stealing inventory for personal use or for sale, stealing scrap for resale, or colluding with a competitor by disclosing technological data in return for payment)
- Causing an entity to pay for goods and services not received (for example, payments to fictitious vendors, kickbacks paid by vendors to the entity's purchasing agents in return for approving payment at inflated prices, or payments to fictitious employees)

---

[16] Paragraph .12 of section 200.

- Using an entity's assets for personal use (for example, using the entity's assets as collateral for a personal loan or a loan to a related party)

Misappropriation of assets is often accompanied by false or misleading records or documents in order to conceal the fact that the assets are missing or have been pledged without proper authorization.

Considerations Specific to Governmental Entities and Not-for-Profit Organizations

.A8 The auditor of governmental entities and not-for-profit organizations may have additional responsibilities relating to fraud

- as a result of being engaged to conduct an audit in accordance with law or regulation applicable to governmental entities and not-for-profit organizations,
- because of a governmental audit organization's mandate, or
- because of the need to comply with *Government Auditing Standards*.

Consequently, the responsibilities of the auditor of governmental entities and not-for-profit organizations may not be limited to consideration of risks of material misstatement of the financial statements, but may also include a broader responsibility to consider risks of fraud.

Professional Skepticism (Ref: par. .12–.14)

.A9 Maintaining professional skepticism requires an ongoing questioning of whether the information and audit evidence obtained suggests that a material misstatement due to fraud may exist. It includes considering the reliability of the information to be used as audit evidence and the controls over its preparation and maintenance when relevant. Due to the characteristics of fraud, the auditor's professional skepticism is particularly important when considering the risks of material misstatement due to fraud.

.A10 Although the auditor cannot be expected to disregard past experience of the honesty and integrity of the entity's management and those charged with governance, the auditor's professional skepticism is particularly important in considering the risks of material misstatement due to fraud because there may have been changes in circumstances.

.A11 An audit performed in accordance with GAAS rarely involves the authentication of documents, nor is the auditor trained as, or expected to be, an expert in such authentication.[17] However, when the auditor identifies conditions that cause the auditor to believe that a document may not be authentic, that terms in a document have been modified but not disclosed to the auditor, or that undisclosed side agreements may exist, possible procedures to investigate further may include

- confirming directly with the third party.
- using the work of a specialist to assess the document's authenticity.

Appendix C, "Examples of Circumstances That Indicate the Possibility of Fraud," contains examples of circumstances that may indicate the possibility of fraud.

---

[17] Paragraph .A51 of section 200.

Discussion Among the Engagement Team (Ref: par. .15)

.A12 Discussing the susceptibility of the entity's financial statements to material misstatement due to fraud with the engagement team

- provides an opportunity for more experienced engagement team members to share their insights about how and where the financial statements may be susceptible to material misstatement due to fraud.
- enables the auditor to consider an appropriate response to such susceptibility and to determine which members of the engagement team will conduct certain audit procedures.
- permits the auditor to determine how the results of audit procedures will be shared among the engagement team and how to deal with any allegations of fraud that may come to the auditor's attention during the audit.

.A13 The discussion may lead to a thorough probing of the issues, acquiring of additional evidence as necessary, and consulting with other team members and, if appropriate, specialists in or outside the firm. The discussion may include the following matters:

- A consideration of management's involvement in overseeing employees with access to cash or other assets susceptible to misappropriation
- A consideration of any unusual or unexplained changes in behavior or lifestyle of management or employees that have come to the attention of the engagement team
- A consideration of the types of circumstances that, if encountered, might indicate the possibility of fraud
- A consideration of how an element of unpredictability will be incorporated into the nature, timing, and extent of the audit procedures to be performed
- A consideration of the audit procedures that might be selected to respond to the susceptibility of the entity's financial statements to material misstatement due to fraud and whether certain types of audit procedures are more effective than others
- A consideration of any allegations of fraud that have come to the auditor's attention

A number of factors may influence the extent of the discussion and how it may occur. For example, if the audit involves more than one location, there could be multiple discussions with team members in differing locations. Another factor in planning the discussions is whether to include specialists assigned to the audit team.

Risk Assessment Procedures and Related Activities

Inquiries of Management

Management's Assessment of the Risk of Material Misstatement Due to Fraud (Ref: par. .17*a*)

.A14 Management accepts responsibility for the entity's internal control and for the preparation and fair presentation of the entity's financial statements. Accordingly, it is appropriate for the auditor to make inquiries of management regarding management's own assessment of the risk of fraud and the controls in place to prevent and detect it. The nature, extent, and frequency of management's assessment of such risk and controls may vary from entity to entity. In some entities, management may make detailed assessments on an annual basis or as part of continuous monitoring. In other entities, management's assessment may be less structured and less frequent. The nature, extent, and frequency of management's assessment are relevant to the auditor's understanding of the entity's control environment. For example, the fact that management has not made an assessment of the risk of fraud may, in some circumstances, be indicative of the lack of importance that management places on internal control.

.A15 *Considerations specific to smaller, less complex entities.* In some entities, particularly smaller entities, the focus of management's assessment may be on the risks of employee fraud or misappropriation of assets.

Management's Process for Identifying and Responding to the Risks of Fraud (Ref: par. .17*b*)

.A16 In the case of entities with multiple locations, management's processes may include different levels of monitoring of operating locations or business segments. Management may also have identified particular operating locations or business segments for which a risk of fraud may be more likely to exist.

Discussions With Management and Others Within the Entity (Ref: par. .17–.19)

.A17 Inquiries of management and others within the entity are generally most effective when they involve an in-person discussion. The auditor may also determine it useful to provide the interviewee with specific questions and obtain written responses in advance of the discussion.

.A18 The auditor's inquiries of management may provide useful information concerning the risks of material misstatements in the financial statements resulting from employee fraud. However, such inquiries are unlikely to provide useful information regarding the risks of material misstatement in the financial statements resulting from management fraud. Making inquiries of others within the entity, in addition to management, may provide individuals with an opportunity to convey information to the auditor that may not otherwise be communicated. It may be useful in providing the auditor with a perspective that is different from that of individuals in the financial reporting process. The responses to these other inquiries might serve to corroborate responses received from management or, alternatively, might provide information regarding the possibility of management override of controls. The auditor may also obtain information about how effectively management has communicated standards of ethical behavior throughout the organization.

.A19 Examples of others within the entity to whom the auditor may direct inquiries about the existence or suspicion of fraud include the following:

- Operating personnel not directly involved in the financial reporting process
- Employees with different levels of authority
- Employees involved in initiating, processing, or recording complex or unusual transactions and those who supervise or monitor such employees
- In-house legal counsel

- Chief ethics officer or equivalent person
- The person or persons charged with dealing with allegations of fraud

.A20 Management is often in the best position to perpetrate fraud. Accordingly, when evaluating management's responses to inquiries with professional skepticism, the auditor may judge it necessary to corroborate responses to inquiries with other information.

Obtaining an Understanding of Oversight Exercised by Those Charged With Governance (Ref: par. .20)

.A21 Those charged with governance of an entity oversee the entity's systems for monitoring risk, financial control, and compliance with the law. In some circumstances, governance practices are well developed, and those charged with governance play an active role in oversight of the entity's assessment of the risks of fraud and of the relevant internal control. Because the responsibilities of those charged with governance and management may vary by entity, it is important that the auditor understands the respective responsibilities of those charged with governance and management to enable the auditor to obtain an understanding of the oversight exercised by the appropriate individuals.[18]

.A22 An understanding of the oversight exercised by those charged with governance may provide insights regarding the susceptibility of the entity to management fraud, the adequacy of internal control over risks of fraud, and the competency and integrity of management. The auditor may obtain this understanding in a number of ways, such as by attending meetings during which such discussions take place, reading the minutes from such meetings, or making inquiries of those charged with governance.

Considerations Specific to Smaller, Less Complex Entities

.A23 In some cases, all of those charged with governance are involved in managing the entity. This may be the case in a small entity in which a single owner manages the entity, and no one else has a governance role. In these cases, ordinarily, no action exists on the part of the auditor because no oversight exists separate from management.

Unusual or Unexpected Relationships Identified (Ref: par. .22)

.A24 Analytical procedures may include data analysis techniques ranging from a high-level review of data patterns, relationships, and trends to highly sophisticated, computer-assisted investigation of detailed transactions using electronic tools, such as data mining, business intelligence, and file query tools. The degree of reliance that can be placed on such techniques is a function primarily of the source (for example, financial, nonfinancial), completeness and reliability of the data, the level of disaggregation, and the nature of the analysis.

.A25 Analytical procedures relating to revenue that are performed with the objective of identifying unusual or unexpected relationships that may indicate a material misstatement due to fraudulent financial reporting may include

a. a comparison of sales volume, as determined from recorded revenue amounts, with production capacity. An excess of sales volume over production capacity may be indicative of recording fictitious sales.

---

[18] Paragraphs .A6–.A12 of section 260 discuss with whom the auditor communicates when the entity's governance structure is not well defined.

b. a trend analysis of revenues by month and sales returns by month, during and shortly after the reporting period. This may indicate the existence of undisclosed side agreements with customers involving the return of goods, which, if known, would preclude revenue recognition.

c. a trend analysis of sales by month compared with units shipped. This may identify a material misstatement of recorded revenues.

.A26 Analytical procedures performed during planning may be helpful in identifying the risks of material misstatement due to fraud. However, if such analytical procedures use data aggregated at a high level, generally the results of those analytical procedures provide only a broad initial indication about whether a material misstatement of the financial statements may exist. Accordingly, the results of analytical procedures performed during planning may be considered along with other information gathered by the auditor in identifying the risks of material misstatement due to fraud.

Other Information (Ref: par. .23)

.A27 In addition to information obtained from applying analytical procedures, other information obtained about the entity and its environment may be helpful in identifying the risks of material misstatement due to fraud. The discussion among team members may provide information that is helpful in identifying such risks. In addition, information obtained from the auditor's client acceptance and retention processes, and experience gained on other engagements performed for the entity, for example, engagements to review interim financial information, may be relevant in the identification of the risks of material misstatement due to fraud.

Evaluation of Fraud Risk Factors (Ref: par. .24)

.A28 The fact that fraud is usually concealed can make it very difficult to detect. Nevertheless, the auditor may identify events or conditions that indicate an incentive or pressure to commit fraud or provide an opportunity to commit fraud (fraud risk factors), such as the following:

- The need to meet expectations of third parties to obtain additional equity financing may create pressure to commit fraud.
- The granting of significant bonuses if unrealistic profit targets are met may create an incentive to commit fraud.
- A control environment that is not effective may create an opportunity to commit fraud.

.A29 Fraud risk factors cannot easily be ranked in order of importance. The significance of fraud risk factors varies widely. Some of these factors will be present in entities in which the specific conditions do not present risks of material misstatement. Accordingly, the determination of whether a fraud risk factor is present and whether it is to be considered in assessing the risks of material misstatement of the financial statements due to fraud requires the exercise of professional judgment.

.A30 Examples of fraud risk factors related to fraudulent financial reporting and misappropriation of assets are presented in appendix A, "Examples of Fraud Risk Factors." These illustrative risk factors are classified based on the three conditions that are generally present when fraud exists:

- An incentive or pressure to commit fraud

- A perceived opportunity to commit fraud
- An ability to rationalize the fraudulent action

The inability to observe one or more of these conditions does not necessarily mean that no risk of material misstatement due to fraud exists.

Risk factors reflective of an attitude that permits rationalization of the fraudulent action may not be susceptible to observation by the auditor. Nevertheless, the auditor may become aware of the existence of such information. Although the fraud risk factors described in appendix A cover a broad range of situations that may be faced by auditors, they are only examples and other risk factors may exist.

.A31 The size, complexity, and ownership characteristics of the entity have a significant influence on the consideration of relevant fraud risk factors. For example, in the case of a large entity, there may be factors that generally constrain improper conduct by management, such as

- effective oversight by those charged with governance.
- an effective internal audit function.
- the existence and enforcement of a written code of conduct.

Furthermore, fraud risk factors considered at a business segment operating level may provide different insights when compared with those obtained when considered at an entity-wide level.

Considerations Specific to Smaller, Less Complex Entities

.A32 In the case of a small entity, some or all of these considerations may be inapplicable or less relevant. For example, a smaller entity may not have a written code of conduct but, instead, may have developed a culture that emphasizes the importance of integrity and ethical behavior through oral communication and by management example. Domination of management by a single individual in a small entity does not generally, in and of itself, indicate a failure by management to display and communicate an appropriate attitude regarding internal control and the financial reporting process. In some entities, the need for management authorization can compensate for otherwise deficient controls and reduce the risk of employee fraud. However, domination of management by a single individual can be a potential deficiency in internal control because an opportunity exists for management override of controls.

Identification and Assessment of the Risks of Material Misstatement Due to Fraud

Risks of Fraud in Revenue Recognition (Ref: par. .26)

.A33 Material misstatement due to fraudulent financial reporting relating to revenue recognition often results from an overstatement of revenues through, for example, premature revenue recognition or recording fictitious revenues. It may result also from an understatement of revenues through, for example, improperly shifting revenues to a later period.

.A34 The risks of fraud in revenue recognition may be greater in some entities than others. For example, there may be pressures or incentives on management to commit fraudulent financial reporting through inappropriate revenue recognition when, for example, performance is measured in terms of year over year revenue growth or profit. Similarly, for example, there may be greater risks of fraud in revenue recognition in the case of entities that generate a substantial portion of revenues through cash sales.

.A35 The presumption that risks of fraud exist in revenue recognition may be rebutted. For example, the auditor may conclude that no risk of material misstatement due to fraud relating to revenue recognition exists in the case in which a single type of simple revenue transaction exists, for example, leasehold revenue from a single unit rental property.

Identifying and Assessing the Risks of Material Misstatement Due to Fraud and Understanding the Entity's Related Controls (Ref: par. .27)

.A36 Management may make judgments on the nature and extent of the controls it chooses to implement, and the nature and extent of the risks it chooses to assume.[19] In determining which controls to implement to prevent and detect fraud, management considers the risks that the financial statements may be materially misstated as a result of fraud. As part of this consideration, management may conclude that it is not cost effective to implement and maintain a particular control in relation to the reduction in the risks of material misstatement due to fraud to be achieved.

.A37 It is, therefore, important for the auditor to obtain an understanding of the controls that management has designed, implemented, and maintained to prevent and detect fraud. In doing so, the auditor may learn, for example, that management has consciously chosen to accept the risks associated with a lack of segregation of duties. Information from obtaining this understanding may also be useful in identifying fraud risks factors that may affect the auditor's assessment of the risks that the financial statements may contain material misstatement due to fraud.

Responses to the Assessed Risks of Material Misstatement Due to Fraud

Overall Responses (Ref: par. .28)

.A38 Determining overall responses to address the assessed risks of material misstatement due to fraud generally includes the consideration of how the overall conduct of the audit can reflect increased professional skepticism through, for example, increased

- sensitivity in the selection of the nature and extent of documentation to be examined in support of material transactions.
- recognition of the need to corroborate management explanations or representations concerning material matters.

Determining overall responses to address the assessed risks of material misstatement due to fraud also involves more general considerations apart from the specific procedures otherwise planned; these considerations include the matters listed in paragraph .29, which are discussed in the following sections.

Assignment and Supervision of Personnel (Ref: par. .29a)

.A39 The auditor may respond to identified risks of material misstatement due to fraud by, for example, assigning additional individuals with specialized skill and knowledge, such as forensic and IT specialists, or by assigning more experienced individuals to the engagement.

.A40 The extent of supervision reflects the auditor's assessment of risks of material misstatement due to fraud and the competencies of the engagement team members performing the work.

---

[19] Paragraph .A48 of section 315.

Accounting Principles (Ref: par. .29b)

.A41 Management bias in the selection and application of accounting principles may individually or collectively involve matters such as contingencies, fair value measurements, revenue recognition, accounting estimates, related party transactions, or other transactions without a clear business purpose.

Unpredictability in the Selection of Audit Procedures (Ref: par. .29c)

.A42 Incorporating an element of unpredictability in the selection of the nature, timing, and extent of audit procedures to be performed is important because individuals within the entity who are familiar with the audit procedures normally performed on engagements may be better able to conceal fraudulent financial reporting. This can be achieved by, for example,

- performing substantive procedures on selected account balances and assertions not otherwise tested due to their materiality or risk.
- adjusting the timing of audit procedures from that otherwise expected.
- using different sampling methods.
- performing audit procedures at different locations or at locations on an unannounced basis.

Audit Procedures Responsive to Assessed Risks of Material Misstatement Due to Fraud at the Assertion Level (Ref: par. .30)

.A43 The auditor's responses to address the assessed risks of material misstatement due to fraud at the assertion level may include changing the nature, timing, and extent of audit procedures in the following ways:

- The nature of audit procedures to be performed may need to be changed to obtain audit evidence that is more reliable and relevant or to obtain additional corroborative information. This may affect both the type of audit procedures to be performed and their combination. For example:
    - — Physical observation or inspection of certain assets may become more important, or the auditor may choose to use computer-assisted audit techniques to gather more evidence about data contained in significant accounts or electronic transaction files.
    - — The auditor may design procedures to obtain additional corroborative information. For example, if the auditor identifies that management is under pressure to meet earnings expectations, there may be a related risk that management is inflating sales by entering into sales agreements that include terms that preclude revenue recognition or by invoicing sales before delivery. In these circumstances, the auditor may, for example, design external confirmations not only to confirm outstanding amounts, but also to confirm the details of the sales agreements, including date, any rights of return, and delivery terms. In addition, the auditor might find it effective to supplement such external confirmations with inquiries of nonfinancial

personnel in the entity regarding any changes in sales agreements and delivery terms.

- The timing of substantive procedures may need to be modified. The auditor may conclude that performing substantive testing at or near the period end better addresses an assessed risk of material misstatement due to fraud. The auditor may conclude that, given the assessed risks of intentional misstatement or manipulation, audit procedures to extend audit conclusions from an interim date to the period end would not be effective. In contrast, because an intentional misstatement—for example, a misstatement involving improper revenue recognition—may have been initiated in an interim period, the auditor may elect to apply substantive procedures to transactions occurring earlier in or throughout the reporting period.

- The extent of the procedures applied reflects the assessment of the risks of material misstatement due to fraud. For example, increasing sample sizes or performing analytical procedures at a more detailed level may be appropriate. Also, computer-assisted audit techniques may enable more extensive testing of electronic transactions and account files. Such techniques can be used to select sample transactions from key electronic files, to sort transactions with specific characteristics, or to test an entire population instead of a sample.

.A44 If the auditor identifies a risk of material misstatement due to fraud that affects inventory quantities, examining the entity's inventory records may help to identify locations or items that require specific attention during or after the physical inventory count. Such a review may lead to a decision to observe inventory counts at certain locations on an unannounced basis or to conduct inventory counts at all locations on the same date.

.A45 The auditor may identify a risk of material misstatement due to fraud affecting a number of accounts and assertions. These may include asset valuation, estimates relating to specific transactions (such as acquisitions, restructurings, or disposals of segments of the business), and other significant accrued liabilities (such as pension and other postemployment benefit obligations, or environmental remediation liabilities). The risk may also relate to significant changes in assumptions relating to recurring estimates. Information gathered through obtaining an understanding of the entity and its environment may assist the auditor in evaluating the reasonableness of such management estimates and underlying judgments and assumptions. A retrospective review of similar management judgments and assumptions applied in prior periods may also provide insight about the reasonableness of judgments and assumptions supporting management estimates.

.A46 Examples of possible audit procedures to address the assessed risks of material misstatement due to fraud, including those that illustrate the incorporation of an element of unpredictability, are presented in appendix B, "Examples of Possible Audit Procedures to Address the Assessed Risks of Material Misstatement Due to Fraud." The appendix includes examples of responses to the auditor's assessment of the risks of material misstatement resulting from both fraudulent financial reporting, including fraudulent financial reporting resulting from revenue recognition, and misappropriation of assets.

Audit Procedures Responsive to Risks Related to Management Override of Controls

Journal Entries and Other Adjustments (Ref: par. .32a)

.A47 Material misstatements of financial statements due to fraud often involve the manipulation of the financial reporting process by (*a*) recording inappropriate or unauthorized journal entries throughout the year or at period end, or (*b*) making adjustments to amounts reported in the financial statements that are not reflected in formal journal entries, such as through consolidating adjustments, report combinations, and reclassifications.

.A48 The auditor's consideration of the risks of material misstatement associated with inappropriate override of controls over journal entries is important because automated processes and controls may reduce the risk of inadvertent error but do not overcome the risk that individuals may inappropriately override such automated processes, for example, by changing the amounts being automatically passed to the general ledger or to the financial reporting system. Furthermore, when IT is used to transfer information automatically, there may be little or no visible evidence of such intervention in the information systems.

.A49 When identifying and selecting journal entries and other adjustments for testing and determining the appropriate method of examining the underlying support for the items selected, the following matters may be relevant:

- *The assessment of the risks of material misstatement due to fraud.* The presence of fraud risk factors and other information obtained during the auditor's assessment of the risks of material misstatement due to fraud may assist the auditor to identify specific classes of journal entries and other adjustments for testing.
- *Controls that have been implemented over journal entries and other adjustments.* Effective controls over the preparation and posting of journal entries and other adjustments may reduce the extent of substantive testing necessary, provided that the auditor has tested the operating effectiveness of the controls.
- *The entity's financial reporting process and the nature of evidence that can be obtained.* For many entities, routine processing of transactions involves a combination of manual and automated steps and procedures. Similarly, the processing of journal entries and other adjustments may involve both manual and automated procedures and controls. When IT is used in the financial reporting process, journal entries and other adjustments may exist only in electronic form.
- *The characteristics of fraudulent journal entries or other adjustments.* Inappropriate journal entries or other adjustments often have unique identifying characteristics. Such characteristics may include entries (*a*) made to unrelated, unusual, or seldom-used accounts; (*b*) made by individuals who typically do not make journal entries; (*c*) recorded at the end of the period or as postclosing entries that have little or no explanation or description; (*d*) made either before or during the preparation of the financial statements that do not have account numbers; or (*e*) containing round numbers or consistent ending numbers.
- *The nature and complexity of the accounts.* Inappropriate journal entries or adjustments may be applied to accounts that (*a*) contain

transactions that are complex or unusual in nature, (*b*) contain significant estimates and period-end adjustments, (*c*) have been prone to misstatements in the past, (*d*) have not been reconciled on a timely basis or contain unreconciled differences, (*e*) contain intercompany transactions, or (*f*) are otherwise associated with an identified risk of material misstatement due to fraud. In audits of entities that have several locations or components, consideration is given to the need to select journal entries from multiple locations.

- *Journal entries or other adjustments processed outside the normal course of business.* Nonstandard journal entries, and other entries such as consolidating adjustments, may not be subject to the same level of internal control as those journal entries used on a recurring basis to record transactions such as monthly sales, purchases, and cash disbursements.

.A50 The auditor exercises professional judgment in determining the nature, timing, and extent of testing of journal entries and other adjustments. However, because fraudulent journal entries and other adjustments are often made at the end of a reporting period, paragraph .32*a*(iv) requires the auditor to select the journal entries and other adjustments made at that time. Further, because material misstatements in financial statements due to fraud can occur throughout the period and may involve extensive efforts to conceal how the fraud is accomplished, paragraph .32*a*(v) requires the auditor to consider whether a need also exists to test journal entries and other adjustments throughout the period.

Accounting Estimates (Ref: par. .32*b*)

.A51 The preparation and fair presentation of the financial statements requires management to make a number of judgments or assumptions that affect significant accounting estimates and monitor the reasonableness of such estimates on an ongoing basis. Fraudulent financial reporting is often accomplished through intentional misstatement of accounting estimates. This may be achieved by, for example, understating or overstating all provisions or reserves in the same fashion so as to be designed either to smooth earnings over two or more accounting periods, or to achieve a designated earnings level in order to deceive financial statement users by influencing their perceptions about the entity's performance and profitability.

.A52 The purpose of performing a retrospective review of management judgments and assumptions related to significant accounting estimates reflected in the financial statements of the prior year is to determine whether an indication exists of a possible bias on the part of management. This review is not intended to call into question the auditor's professional judgments made in the prior year that were based on information available at the time.

.A53 A retrospective review is also required by section 540, *Auditing Accounting Estimates, Including Fair Value Accounting Estimates, and Related Disclosures.*[20] That review is conducted as a risk assessment procedure to obtain information regarding the effectiveness of management's prior period estimation process, audit evidence about the outcome, or when applicable, the subsequent reestimation of prior period accounting estimates that is pertinent to making current period accounting estimates, and audit evidence of matters,

---

[20] Paragraph .09 of section 540, *Auditing Accounting Estimates, Including Fair Value Accounting Estimates, and Related Disclosures.*

such as estimation uncertainty, that may be required to be disclosed in the financial statements. As a practical matter, the auditor's review of management judgments and assumptions for biases that could represent a risk of material misstatement due to fraud in accordance with this section may be carried out in conjunction with the review required by section 540.

Business Rationale for Significant Transactions (Ref: par. .32c)

.A54 Indicators that may suggest that significant transactions that are outside the normal course of business for the entity, or that otherwise appear to be unusual, may have been entered into to engage in fraudulent financial reporting or to conceal misappropriation of assets include the following:

- The form of such transactions appears overly complex (for example, the transaction involves multiple entities within a consolidated group or multiple unrelated third parties).
- Management has not discussed the nature of and accounting for such transactions with those charged with governance of the entity, and inadequate documentation exists.
- Management is placing more emphasis on the need for a particular accounting treatment than on the underlying economics of the transaction.
- Transactions that involve nonconsolidated related parties, including special purpose entities, have not been properly reviewed or approved by those charged with governance of the entity.
- Transactions that involve previously unidentified related parties or parties that do not have the substance or the financial strength to support the transaction without assistance from the entity under audit.

Other Audit Procedures (Ref: par. .32a and .33)

.A55 Risks of material misstatement, including misstatements due to fraud, cannot be reduced to an appropriately low level by performing only tests of controls.[21]

Evaluation of Audit Evidence (Ref: par. .34–.37)

.A56 Section 330 requires the auditor, based on the audit procedures performed and the audit evidence obtained, to evaluate whether the assessments of the risks of material misstatement at the assertion level remain appropriate.[22] This evaluation is primarily a qualitative matter based on the auditor's professional judgment. Such an evaluation may provide further insight into the risks of material misstatement due to fraud and whether a need exists to perform additional or different audit procedures. Appendix C contains examples of circumstances that may indicate the possibility of fraud.

Analytical Procedures Performed Near the End of the Audit in Forming an Overall Conclusion (Ref: par. .34)

.A57 Determining which particular trends and relationships may indicate a risk of material misstatement due to fraud requires professional judgment. Unusual relationships involving year-end revenue and income are particularly relevant. These might include, for example, uncharacteristically large amounts

---

[21] Paragraph .A9 of section 330.

[22] Paragraph .27 of section 330.

of income being reported in the last few weeks of the reporting period or unusual transactions or income that is inconsistent with trends in cash flow from operations.

.A58 Some unusual or unexpected analytical relationships may have been identified and may indicate a risk of material misstatement due to fraud because management or employees generally are unable to manipulate certain information to create seemingly normal or expected relationships. Some examples are as follows:

- The relationship of net income to cash flows from operations may appear unusual because management recorded fictitious revenues and receivables but was unable to manipulate cash.
- Changes in inventory, accounts payable, sales, or cost of sales from the prior period to the current period may be inconsistent, indicating a possible employee theft of inventory, because the employee was unable to manipulate all of the related accounts.
- A comparison of the entity's profitability to industry trends, which management cannot manipulate, may indicate trends or differences for further consideration when identifying risks of material misstatement due to fraud.
- A comparison of bad debt write-offs to comparable industry data, which employees cannot manipulate, may provide unexplained relationships that could indicate a possible theft of cash receipts.
- An unexpected or unexplained relationship between sales volume, as determined from the accounting records and production statistics maintained by operations personnel, which may be more difficult for management to manipulate, may indicate a possible misstatement of sales.

Consideration of Identified Misstatements (Ref: par. .35–.37)

.A59 Because fraud involves incentive or pressure to commit fraud, a perceived opportunity to do so, or some rationalization of the act, an instance of fraud is unlikely to be an isolated occurrence. Accordingly, misstatements, such as numerous misstatements at a specific location even though the cumulative effect is not material, may be indicative of a risk of material misstatement due to fraud.

.A60 The implications of identified fraud depend on the circumstances. For example, an otherwise insignificant fraud may be significant if it involves senior management. In such circumstances, the reliability of evidence previously obtained may be called into question because there may be doubts about the completeness and truthfulness of representations made and the genuineness of accounting records and documentation. There may also be a possibility of collusion involving employees, management, or third parties.

.A61 Section 450, *Evaluation of Misstatements Identified During the Audit*, and section 700, *Forming an Opinion and Reporting on Financial Statements*, address the evaluation and disposition of misstatements and the effect on the auditor's opinion in the auditor's report.

.A62 Section 580, *Written Representations*, addresses obtaining appropriate representations from management in the audit. In addition to acknowledging its responsibility for the financial statements, it is important that, irrespective of the size of the entity, management acknowledges its responsibility for internal control designed, implemented, and maintained to prevent and detect fraud.

Auditor Unable to Continue the Engagement (Ref: par. .38)

.A63 Examples of circumstances that may arise and bring into question the auditor's ability to continue performing the audit include the following:

a. The entity does not take the appropriate action regarding fraud that the auditor considers necessary in the circumstances, even when the fraud is not material to the financial statements.

b. The auditor's consideration of the risks of material misstatement due to fraud and the results of audit tests indicate a significant risk of material and pervasive fraud.

c. The auditor has significant concern about the competence or integrity of management or those charged with governance.

.A64 Because of the variety of circumstances that may arise, it is not possible to describe definitively when withdrawal from an engagement is appropriate. Factors that affect the auditor's conclusion include the implications of the involvement of a member of management or of those charged with governance (which may affect the reliability of management representations) and the effects on the auditor of a continuing association with the entity.

.A65 The auditor has professional and legal responsibilities in such circumstances, and these responsibilities may vary by engagement. In some circumstances, for example, the auditor may be entitled to, or required to, make a statement or report to the person or persons who engaged the auditor or, in some cases, to regulatory authorities. Given the nature of the circumstances and the need to consider the legal requirements, the auditor may consider it appropriate to seek legal advice when deciding whether to withdraw from an engagement and in determining an appropriate course of action, including the possibility of reporting to regulators or others.[23]

Considerations Specific to Governmental Entities and Not-for-Profit Organizations

.A66 For governmental entities and not-for-profit organizations, the option of withdrawing from the engagement may not be available to the auditor due to the nature of the mandate, public interest considerations, contractual requirements, or law or regulation.

Communications to Management and With Those Charged With Governance

Communication to Management (Ref: par. .39)

.A67 When the auditor has obtained evidence that fraud exists or may exist, it is important that the matter be brought to the attention of the appropriate level of management as soon as practicable. This is true even if the matter might be considered inconsequential (for example, a minor defalcation by an employee at a low level in the entity's organization). The determination of which level of management is the appropriate one is a matter of professional judgment and is affected by such factors as the likelihood of collusion and the nature and magnitude of the suspected fraud. Ordinarily, the appropriate level of management is at least one level above the persons who appear to be involved with the suspected fraud.

---

[23] Section 510, *Opening Balances—Initial Audit Engagements, Including Reaudit Engagements*, provides guidance on communications with an auditor replacing the existing auditor.

Communication With Those Charged With Governance (Ref: par. .40)

.A68 The auditor's communication with those charged with governance may be made orally or in writing. Section 260, *The Auditor's Communication With Those Charged With Governance*, identifies factors the auditor considers in determining whether to communicate orally or in writing.[24] Due to the nature and sensitivity of fraud involving senior management, or fraud that results in a material misstatement in the financial statements, the auditor communicates such matters on a timely basis and may consider it necessary to also communicate such matters in writing.

.A69 In some cases, the auditor may consider it appropriate to communicate with those charged with governance when the auditor becomes aware of fraud involving employees other than management that does not result in a material misstatement. Similarly, those charged with governance may wish to be informed of such circumstances. The communication process is assisted if the auditor and those charged with governance agree at an early stage in the audit about the nature and extent of the auditor's communications in this regard.

.A70 When the auditor has doubts about the integrity or honesty of management or those charged with governance, the auditor may consider it appropriate to obtain legal advice to assist in determining the appropriate course of action.

Other Matters Related to Fraud (Ref: par. .41)

.A71 Other matters related to fraud to be discussed with those charged with governance of the entity may include, for example

- concerns about the nature, extent, and frequency of management's assessments of the controls in place to prevent and detect fraud and of the risk that the financial statements may be misstated.
- a failure by management to appropriately address identified significant deficiencies or material weaknesses in internal control, or to appropriately respond to an identified fraud.
- the auditor's evaluation of the entity's control environment, including questions regarding the competence and integrity of management.
- actions by management that may be indicative of fraudulent financial reporting, such as management's selection and application of accounting policies that may be indicative of management's effort to manage earnings in order to deceive financial statement users by influencing their perceptions concerning the entity's performance and profitability.
- concerns about the adequacy and completeness of the authorization of transactions that appear to be outside the normal course of business.
- the absence of programs or controls to address risks of material misstatement due to fraud that are significant deficiencies or material weaknesses.[25]

---

[24] Paragraph .A40 of section 260.

[25] See section 265, *Communicating Internal Control Related Matters Identified in an Audit*.

Communications to Regulatory and Enforcement Authorities (Ref: par. .42)

.A72 The auditor's professional duty to maintain the confidentiality of client information may preclude reporting fraud to a party outside the client entity. However, in certain circumstances, the duty of confidentiality may be overridden by statute, regulation, courts of law, specific requirements of audits of entities that receive government financial assistance, or waived by agreement. In some circumstances, the auditor has a statutory duty to report the occurrence of fraud to supervisory authorities. Also, in some circumstances, the auditor has a duty to report misstatements to authorities in those cases when management and those charged with governance fail to take corrective action.

.A73 The auditor may consider it appropriate to obtain legal advice to determine the appropriate course of action in the circumstances, the purpose of which is to ascertain the steps necessary in considering the public interest aspects of identified fraud.

Considerations Specific to Governmental Entities and Not-for-Profit Organizations

.A74 For governmental entities and not-for-profit organizations, requirements for reporting fraud, whether or not discovered through the audit process, may be subject to specific provisions of the audit mandate or related law or regulation.

.A75

Appendix A—Examples of Fraud Risk Factors (Ref: par. .11, .24, and .A30)

The fraud risk factors identified in this appendix are examples of such factors that may be faced by auditors in a broad range of situations. Separately presented are examples relating to the two types of fraud relevant to the auditor's consideration—that is, fraudulent financial reporting and misappropriation of assets. For each of these types of fraud, the risk factors are further classified based on the three conditions generally present when material misstatements due to fraud occur: (*a*) incentives and pressures, (*b*) opportunities, and (*c*) attitudes and rationalizations. Although the risk factors cover a broad range of situations, they are only examples and, accordingly, the auditor may identify additional or different risk factors. Not all of these examples are relevant in all circumstances, and some may be of greater or lesser significance in entities of different size or with different ownership characteristics or circumstances. Also, the order of the examples of risk factors provided is not intended to reflect their relative importance or frequency of occurrence.

Risk Factors Relating to Misstatements Arising From Fraudulent Financial Reporting

The following are examples of risk factors relating to misstatements arising from fraudulent financial reporting.

Incentives and Pressures

Financial stability or profitability is threatened by economic, industry, or entity operating conditions, such as (or as indicated by) the following:

- High degree of competition or market saturation, accompanied by declining margins
- High vulnerability to rapid changes, such as changes in technology, product obsolescence, or interest rates
- Significant declines in customer demand and increasing business failures in either the industry or overall economy
- Operating losses making the threat of bankruptcy, foreclosure, or hostile takeover imminent
- Recurring negative cash flows from operations or an inability to generate cash flows from operations while reporting earnings and earnings growth
- Rapid growth or unusual profitability especially compared to that of other companies in the same industry
- New accounting, statutory, or regulatory requirements

Excessive pressure exists for management to meet the requirements or expectations of third parties due to the following:

- Profitability or trend level expectations of investment analysts, institutional investors, significant creditors, or other external parties (particularly expectations that are unduly aggressive or unrealistic), including expectations created by management in, for example, overly optimistic press releases or annual report messages

- Need to obtain additional debt or equity financing to stay competitive—including financing of major research and development or capital expenditures
- Marginal ability to meet exchange listing requirements or debt repayment or other debt covenant requirements
- Perceived or real adverse effects of reporting poor financial results on significant pending transactions, such as business combinations or contract awards
- A need to achieve financial targets required in bond covenants
- Pressure for management to meet the expectations of legislative or oversight bodies or to achieve political outcomes, or both

Information available indicates that the personal financial situation of management or those charged with governance is threatened by the entity's financial performance arising from the following:

- Significant financial interests in the entity
- Significant portions of their compensation (for example, bonuses, stock options, and earn-out arrangements) being contingent upon achieving aggressive targets for stock price, operating results, financial position, or cash flow[1]
- Personal guarantees of debts of the entity

Management or operating personnel are under excessive pressure to meet financial targets established by those charged with governance, including sales or profitability incentive goals.

Opportunities

The nature of the industry or the entity's operations provides opportunities to engage in fraudulent financial reporting that can arise from the following:

- Significant related party transactions not in the ordinary course of business or with related entities not audited or audited by another firm
- A strong financial presence or ability to dominate a certain industry sector that allows the entity to dictate terms or conditions to suppliers or customers that may result in inappropriate or non-arm's-length transactions
- Assets, liabilities, revenues, or expenses based on significant estimates that involve subjective judgments or uncertainties that are difficult to corroborate
- Significant, unusual, or highly complex transactions, especially those close to period end that pose difficult "substance over form" questions
- Significant operations located or conducted across jurisdictional borders where differing business environments and regulations exist

---

[1] Management incentive plans may be contingent upon achieving targets relating only to certain accounts or selected activities of the entity, even though the related accounts or activities may not be material to the entity as a whole.

- Use of business intermediaries for which there appears to be no clear business justification
- Significant bank accounts or subsidiary or branch operations in tax-haven jurisdictions for which there appears to be no clear business justification

The monitoring of management is not effective as a result of the following:

- Domination of management by a single person or small group (in a nonowner-managed business) without compensating controls.
- Oversight by those charged with governance over the financial reporting process and internal control is not effective.

The organizational structure is complex or unstable, as evidenced by the following:

- Difficulty in determining the organization or individuals that have controlling interest in the entity
- Overly complex organizational structure involving unusual legal entities or managerial lines of authority
- High turnover of senior management, legal counsel, or those charged with governance

Internal control components are deficient as a result of the following:

- Inadequate monitoring of controls, including automated controls and controls over interim financial reporting (when external reporting is required)
- High turnover rates or employment of accounting, internal audit, or IT staff who are not effective
- Accounting and information systems that are not effective, including situations involving significant deficiencies or material weaknesses in internal control
- Weak controls over budget preparation and development and compliance with law or regulation.

Attitudes and Rationalizations

- Communication, implementation, support, or enforcement of the entity's values or ethical standards by management, or the communication of inappropriate values or ethical standards that are not effective.
- Nonfinancial management's excessive participation in or preoccupation with the selection of accounting policies or the determination of significant estimates.
- Known history of violations of securities law or other law or regulation, or claims against the entity, its senior management, or those charged with governance alleging fraud or violations of law or regulation.
- Excessive interest by management in maintaining or increasing the entity's stock price or earnings trend.
- The practice by management of committing to analysts, creditors, and other third parties to achieve aggressive or unrealistic forecasts.

- Management failing to remedy known significant deficiencies or material weaknesses in internal control on a timely basis.
- An interest by management in employing inappropriate means to minimize reported earnings for tax-motivated reasons.
- Low morale among senior management.
- The owner-manager makes no distinction between personal and business transactions.
- Dispute between shareholders in a closely held entity.
- Recurring attempts by management to justify marginal or inappropriate accounting on the basis of materiality.
- A strained relationship between management and the current or predecessor auditor, as exhibited by the following:
    - — Frequent disputes with the current or predecessor auditor on accounting, auditing, or reporting matters
    - — Unreasonable demands on the auditor, such as unrealistic time constraints regarding the completion of the audit or the issuance of the auditor's report
    - — Restrictions on the auditor that inappropriately limit access to people or information or the ability to communicate effectively with those charged with governance
    - — Domineering management behavior in dealing with the auditor, especially involving attempts to influence the scope of the auditor's work or the selection or continuance of personnel assigned to or consulted on the audit engagement

Risk Factors Arising From Misstatements Arising From Misappropriation of Assets

Risk factors that relate to misstatements arising from misappropriation of assets are also classified according to the three conditions generally present when fraud exists: incentives and pressures, opportunities, and attitudes and rationalization. Some of the risk factors related to misstatements arising from fraudulent financial reporting also may be present when misstatements arising from misappropriation of assets occur. For example, ineffective monitoring of management and other deficiencies in internal control that are not effective may be present when misstatements due to either fraudulent financial reporting or misappropriation of assets exist. The following are examples of risk factors related to misstatements arising from misappropriation of assets.

Incentives and Pressures

Personal financial obligations may create pressure on management or employees with access to cash or other assets susceptible to theft to misappropriate those assets.

Adverse relationships between the entity and employees with access to cash or other assets susceptible to theft may motivate those employees to misappropriate those assets. For example, adverse relationships may be created by the following:

- Known or anticipated future employee layoffs

- Recent or anticipated changes to employee compensation or benefit plans
- Promotions, compensation, or other rewards inconsistent with expectations

Opportunities

Certain characteristics or circumstances may increase the susceptibility of assets to misappropriation. For example, opportunities to misappropriate assets increase when the following exist:

- Large amounts of cash on hand or processed
- Inventory items that are small in size, of high value, or in high demand
- Easily convertible assets, such as bearer bonds, diamonds, or computer chips
- Fixed assets that are small in size, marketable, or lack observable identification of ownership

Inadequate internal control over assets may increase the susceptibility of misappropriation of those assets. For example, misappropriation of assets may occur because the following exist:

- Inadequate segregation of duties or independent checks
- Inadequate oversight of senior management expenditures, such as travel and other reimbursements
- Inadequate management oversight of employees responsible for assets (for example, inadequate supervision or monitoring of remote locations)
- Inadequate job applicant screening of employees with access to assets
- Inadequate record keeping with respect to assets
- Inadequate system of authorization and approval of transactions (for example, in purchasing)
- Inadequate physical safeguards over cash, investments, inventory, or fixed assets
- Lack of complete and timely reconciliations of assets
- Lack of timely and appropriate documentation of transactions (for example, credits for merchandise returns)
- Lack of mandatory vacations for employees performing key control functions
- Inadequate management understanding of IT, which enables IT employees to perpetrate a misappropriation
- Inadequate access controls over automated records, including controls over and review of computer systems event logs

Attitudes and Rationalizations

- Disregard for the need for monitoring or reducing risks related to misappropriations of assets

- Disregard for internal control over misappropriation of assets by overriding existing controls or by failing to take appropriate remedial action on known deficiencies in internal control
- Behavior indicating displeasure or dissatisfaction with the entity or its treatment of the employee
- Changes in behavior or lifestyle that may indicate assets have been misappropriated
- The belief by some government or other officials that their level of authority justifies a certain level of compensation and personal privileges
- Tolerance of petty theft

.A76

Appendix B—Examples of Possible Audit Procedures to Address the Assessed Risks of Material Misstatement Due to Fraud (Ref: par. .22 and .A46)

The following are examples of possible audit procedures to address the assessed risks of material misstatement due to fraud resulting from both fraudulent financial reporting and misappropriation of assets. Although these procedures cover a broad range of situations, they are only examples and, accordingly, they may not be the most appropriate nor necessary in each circumstance. Also the order of the procedures provided is not intended to reflect their relative importance.

Consideration at the Assertion Level

Specific responses to the auditor's assessment of the risks of material misstatement due to fraud will vary depending upon the types or combinations of fraud risk factors or conditions identified, and the classes of transactions, account balances, disclosures, and assertions they may affect.

The following are specific examples of responses:

- Visiting locations or performing certain tests on a surprise or unannounced basis (for example, observing inventory at locations where auditor attendance has not been previously announced or counting cash at a particular date on a surprise basis)
- Requesting that inventories be counted at the end of the reporting period or on a date closer to period end to minimize the risk of manipulation of balances in the period between the date of completion of the count and the end of the reporting period
- Altering the audit approach in the current year (for example, contacting major customers and suppliers orally in addition to sending written confirmation, sending confirmation requests to a specific party within an organization, or seeking more or different information)
- Performing a detailed review of the entity's quarter-end or year-end adjusting entries and investigating any that appear to have an unusual nature or amount
- For significant and unusual transactions, particularly those occurring at or near year end, investigating the possibility of related parties and the sources of financial resources supporting the transactions
- Performing substantive analytical procedures using disaggregated data (for example, comparing sales and cost of sales by location, line of business, or month to expectations developed by the auditor)
- Conducting interviews of personnel involved in areas in which a risk of material misstatement due to fraud has been identified, to obtain their insights about the risk, and whether, or how, controls address the risk
- When other independent auditors are auditing the financial statements of one or more subsidiaries, divisions, or branches,

discussing with them the extent of work necessary to be performed to address the assessed risk of material misstatement due to fraud resulting from transactions and activities among these components

- If the work of an expert becomes particularly significant with respect to a financial statement item for which the assessed risk of misstatement due to fraud is high, performing additional procedures relating to some or all of the expert's assumptions, methods, or findings to determine that the findings are not unreasonable, or engaging another expert for that purpose
- Performing audit procedures to analyze selected opening balance sheet accounts of previously audited financial statements to assess how certain issues involving accounting estimates and judgments, for example, an allowance for sales returns, were resolved with the benefit of hindsight
- Performing procedures on account or other reconciliations prepared by the entity, including considering reconciliations performed at interim periods
- Performing computer-assisted techniques, such as data mining to test for anomalies in a population
- Testing the integrity of computer-produced records and transactions
- Seeking additional audit evidence from sources outside of the entity being audited

Specific Responses—Misstatement Resulting From Fraudulent Financial Reporting

Examples of responses to the auditor's assessment of the risks of material misstatement due to fraudulent financial reporting are as follows:

Revenue Recognition

- Performing substantive analytical procedures relating to revenue using disaggregated data; for example, comparing revenue reported by month and by product line or business segment during the current reporting period with comparable prior periods or with revenue related to cash collections (computer-assisted audit techniques may be useful in identifying unusual or unexpected revenue relationships or transactions)
- Confirming with customers certain relevant contract terms and the absence of side agreements because the appropriate accounting often is influenced by such terms or agreements and basis for rebates or the period to which they relate are often poorly documented (for example, acceptance criteria, delivery and payment terms, the absence of future or continuing vendor obligations, the right to return the product, guaranteed resale amounts, and cancellation or refund provisions often are relevant in such circumstances)
- Inquiring of the entity's sales and marketing personnel or in-house legal counsel regarding sales or shipments near the end of the period and their knowledge of any unusual terms or conditions associated with these transactions

- Being physically present at one or more locations at period end to observe goods being shipped or being readied for shipment (or returns awaiting processing) and performing other appropriate sales and inventory cutoff procedures
- For those situations for which revenue transactions are electronically initiated, processed, and recorded, testing controls to determine whether they provide assurance that recorded revenue transactions occurred and are properly recorded

Inventory Quantities

- Examining the entity's inventory records to identify locations or items that require specific attention during or after the physical inventory count
- Observing inventory counts at certain locations on an unannounced basis or conducting inventory counts at all locations on the same date
- Conducting inventory counts at or near the end of the reporting period to minimize the risk of inappropriate manipulation during the period between the count and the end of the reporting period
- Performing additional procedures during the observation of the count; for example, more rigorously examining the contents of boxed items, the manner in which the goods are stacked (for example, hollow squares) or labeled, and the quality (that is, purity, grade, or concentration) of liquid substances such as perfumes or specialty chemicals (using the work of an expert may be helpful in this regard)
- Comparing the quantities for the current period with prior periods by class or category of inventory, location or other criteria, or comparison of quantities counted with perpetual records
- Using computer-assisted audit techniques to further test the compilation of the physical inventory counts (for example, sorting by tag number to test tag controls or by item serial number to test the possibility of item omission or duplication)

Management Estimates

- Using an expert to develop an independent estimate for comparison to management's estimate
- Extending inquiries to individuals outside of management and the accounting department to corroborate management's ability and intent to carry out plans that are relevant to developing the estimate

Specific Responses—Misstatements Due to Misappropriation of Assets

Differing circumstances would necessarily dictate different responses. Ordinarily, the audit response to an assessed risk of material misstatement due to fraud relating to misappropriation of assets will be directed toward certain account balances and classes of transactions. Although some of the audit responses noted in the preceding two categories may apply in such circumstances, the scope of the work is to be linked to the specific information about the misappropriation risk that has been identified.

Examples of responses to the auditor's assessment of the risk of material misstatements due to misappropriation of assets are as follows:

- Counting cash or securities at or near year end
- Confirming directly with customers the account activity (including credit memo and sales return activity as well as dates payments were made) for the period under audit
- Analyzing recoveries of written-off accounts
- Analyzing inventory shortages by location or product type
- Comparing key inventory ratios to industry norm
- Reviewing supporting documentation for reductions to the perpetual inventory records
- Performing a computerized match of the vendor list with a list of employees to identify matches of addresses or phone numbers
- Performing a computerized search of payroll records to identify duplicate addresses, employee identification or taxing authority numbers, or bank accounts
- Reviewing personnel files for those that contain little or no evidence of activity; for example, lack of performance evaluations
- Analyzing sales discounts and returns for unusual patterns or trends
- Confirming specific terms of contracts with third parties
- Obtaining evidence that contracts are being carried out in accordance with their terms
- Reviewing the propriety of large and unusual expenses
- Reviewing the authorization and carrying value of senior management and related party loans
- Reviewing the level and propriety of expense reports submitted by senior management

.A77

Appendix C—Examples of Circumstances That Indicate the Possibility of Fraud (Ref: par. .11, .A11, and .A56)

The following are examples of circumstances that may indicate the possibility that the financial statements may contain a material misstatement resulting from fraud.

Discrepancies in the accounting records, including the following:

- Transactions that are not recorded in a complete or timely manner or are improperly recorded by amount, accounting period, classification, or entity policy
- Unsupported or unauthorized balances or transactions
- Last minute adjustments that significantly affect financial results
- Evidence of employees' access to systems and records inconsistent with that necessary to perform their authorized duties
- Tips or complaints to the auditor about alleged fraud

Conflicting or missing evidence, including the following:

- Missing documents
- Documents that appear to have been altered
- Unavailability of other than photocopied or electronically transmitted documents when documents in original form are expected to exist
- Significant unexplained items on reconciliations
- Unusual balance sheet changes, or changes in trends or important financial statement ratios or relationships; for example, receivables growing faster than revenues
- Inconsistent, vague, or implausible responses from management or employees arising from inquiries or analytical procedures
- Unusual discrepancies between the entity's records and confirmation replies
- Large numbers of credit entries and other adjustments made to accounts receivable records
- Unexplained or inadequately explained differences between the accounts receivable subledger and the control account, or between the customer statements and the accounts receivable subledger
- Missing or nonexistent cancelled checks in circumstances in which cancelled checks are ordinarily returned to the entity with the bank statement
- Missing inventory or physical assets of significant magnitude
- Unavailable or missing electronic evidence, inconsistent with the entity's record retention practices or policies
- Fewer responses to confirmations than anticipated or a greater number of responses than anticipated

- Inability to produce evidence of key systems development and program change testing and implementation activities for current-year system changes and deployments

Conditions relating to governmental entities or not-for-profit organizations:

- Significant transfers or transactions between funds or programs, or both, lacking supporting documents
- Abnormal budget conditions, such as
  - — significant budget adjustments
  - — requests for additional funding
  - — budget adjustments made without approval
  - — large amounts of over-or-under spending
  - — programs with an emphasis on spending money quickly
- Procurement conditions, such as
  - — lack of procurement legislation
  - — recent changes to procurement legislation
  - — complex or unclear legislation
  - — involvement of significant monetary amounts (such as in the defense area)
  - — investigation by regulatory authorities
  - — complaints received from potential suppliers about questionable practices related to awarding of contracts
  - — former governmental officials functioning as executives of companies to which contracts have been awarded
- Program conditions, such as
  - — newly implemented programs without existing management and accountability structures
  - — programs established for political purposes
  - — programs established to deal with an immediate emergency or crisis
  - — programs experiencing unusual growth due to conditions beyond the control of management
- Grant and donor funding conditions, such as
  - — noncompliance with grant requirements
  - — unclear grant requirements
  - — grants not reaching the intended recipient
  - — complaints from intended recipients or interest groups, and lack of monitoring of grantee compliance with applicable law or regulation

Problematic or unusual relationships between the auditor and management, including the following:

- Denial of access to records, facilities, certain employees, customers, vendors, or others from whom audit evidence might be sought

- Undue time pressures imposed by management to resolve complex or contentious issues
- Complaints by management about the conduct of the audit or management intimidation of engagement team members, particularly in connection with the auditor's critical assessment of audit evidence or in the resolution of potential disagreements with management
- Unusual delays by the entity in providing requested information
- Unwillingness to facilitate auditor access to key electronic files for testing through the use of computer-assisted audit techniques
- Denial of access to key IT operations staff and facilities, including security, operations, and systems development personnel
- An unwillingness to add or revise disclosures in the financial statements to make them more complete and understandable
- An unwillingness to address identified deficiencies in internal control on a timely basis

Other circumstances, including the following:

- Unwillingness by management to permit the auditor to meet privately with those charged with governance
- Accounting policies that appear to be at variance with industry norms
- Frequent changes in accounting estimates that do not appear to result from changed circumstances
- Tolerance of violations of the entity's code of conduct

Appendix B

OTHER SOURCES OF INFORMATION

Other Sources of Information

Other Guidance

A number of resources are available to assist the auditor in obtaining information related to economic, regulatory, and professional developments impacting audits of governmental and not-for-profit organizations. While not exhaustive by any means, auditors may find the following resources helpful in planning and performing audits of governmental and not-for-profit organizations.

AICPA Accounting and Auditing Technical Hotline

Members may inquire about accounting, auditing, attestation, compilation and review services using the Technical Hotline by calling 1.888.777.7077 or 1.877.242.7212.

AICPA Audit and Accounting Guides and Risk Alerts

Separate audit and accounting guides and risk alerts specific to audits of governmental and not-for-profit organizations are available through the AICPA. Obtain by calling the AICPA Order Department 1.888.777.7077 or through www.aicpastore.com.

AICPA Continuing Professional Education Courses

A great number of continuing education courses are available through the AICPA in either group or self-study formats. Information and ordering is available through www.aicpalearning.org.

AICPA Ethics Hotline

Member questions related to independence and other behavioral issues related to the AICPA Code of Professional Conduct may be directed to the Ethics Hotline. Members of the AICPA's Professional Ethics Team may be contacted through the AICPA at 1.888.777.7077.

Financial Accounting Standards Board Publications

FASB publications are available directly from the FASB. Obtain by calling the FASB Order Department at 1.800.748.0659 or through the Internet at www.fasb.org.

Government Accountability Office Publications

Copies of GAO reports and testimony are available directly through the GAO at www.gao.gov.

Governmental Accounting Standards Board Publications

GASB publications are available directly from the GASB. Obtain by calling the GASB Order Department at 1.800.748.0659 or through the Internet at www.gasb.org. Auditors may find the GASB Technical Bulletins issued periodically and the Comprehensive Implementation Guide issued annually helpful in understanding certain specific aspects of governmental accounting and financial reporting.

Government Finance Officers Association

Even though most GFOA publications are written primarily for government finance officers, auditors of governmental organizations may find them helpful. Inquiries may be made by phone 1.312.977.9700, fax 1.312.977.4806, or www.gfoa.org.

Helpful Websites

The Internet is an extremely efficient and effective way in which auditors may access additional information. However, there is a great deal of inconsistency in the reliability of information available through the Internet. Auditors should exercise caution when relying on information obtained through the Internet especially when the source is not well known to the auditor.

Again, the following list is not exhaustive by any means; however, auditors may find the following Internet resources helpful in audits of governmental and not-for-profit organizations.

Organization	Website Address
American College of Forensic Examiners	www.acfei.com
American Institute of CPAs	www.aicpa.org
Association of Certified Fraud Examiners	www.acfe.com
Association of Government Accountants	www.agacgfm.org
Federal Audit Clearinghouse	https://harvester.census.gov/facweb
Federal Chief Financial Officers Council	https://cfo.gov/
Financial Accounting Standards Board	www.fasb.org
Government Accountability Office	www.gao.gov
Government Publishing Office	www.gpo.gov
Government Finance Officers Association	www.gfoa.org
Governmental Accounting Standards Board	www.gasb.org
Healthcare Financial Management Association	www.hfma.org
IGnet (Federal Inspectors General site)	www.ignet.gov
Information Systems Audit and Control Association	www.isaca.org
Institute of Internal Auditors	www.theiia.org
Institute of Management Accountants	www.imanet.org

Organization	Website Address
Internal Revenue Service	www.irs.gov
Municipal Securities Rulemaking Board	www.msrb.org
National Association of Corporate Directors	www.nacdonline.org
National Association of State Auditors, Comptrollers, and Treasurers	www.nasact.org
Society for Human Resource Management	www.shrm.org
United States Government	www.usa.gov
U.S. Office of Management and Budget	www.omb.gov

FRAUD GLOSSARY[1]

Advance Fee Fraud – Falsely obtaining an advance fee for work or services not performed.

Alford Plea – Named after the Supreme Court case that upheld the practice under which a defendant pleads guilty, although continuing to assert innocence. Such a plea may be made to obtain the benefits of a plea agreement and to avoid potentially more dire consequences, such as the death penalty, if the defendant is convicted after trial.

Anti-Kickback Act of 1986 – The provisions of this act are contained in Title 41, U.S. Code, §§ 51-58). The act outlaws the giving or receiving of anything of value for the purpose of improperly obtaining or receiving favorable treatment in connection with U.S. government contracts.

Arbitration – Process whereby the dispute is submitted to an impartial third-person who then decides the outcome of the case, i.e., which party should win. The arbitrator acts as a judge or jury would by deciding the case on its merits. An arbitration can be either "binding" or "nonbinding." If the arbitration is binding, then the decision of the arbitrator is final, and the parties cannot later submit their dispute to a judge or jury for determination.

Arraignment – Because of due process considerations, the defendant has to be brought before the court shortly after his arrest. He enters a plea at this time in a proceeding that is called an *arraignment*. He will be given notice of the charges against him, be informed of his rights, and, if applicable, bail will be set.

Attorney Work Product Doctrine – Under Rule 26(b)(3) of the Federal Rules of Civil Procedure, documents and tangible things which are prepared in anticipation of litigation or for a trial are protected by the work product privilege. The information may be disclosed only if the opposing party can show "substantial need" for the protected information and that the information cannot be obtained from another source. The privilege extends to information prepared by or for a party or the party's representative including attorneys and consultants.

Attorney-Client Privilege – This privilege precludes disclosure of communications between an attorney and client, but only if the following conditions are met: (1) the client retained the attorney, (2) to provide legal advice, (3) and thereafter communicated with the attorney on a confidential basis, and, (4) has not waived the privilege.

Best Evidence Rule – Prohibits a party from testifying about the contents of a document without producing the document itself. Also known as the *"original writing" rule*, it requires that when a witness testifies about the contents of a document, at least a fair copy of the original must be available for inspection. If there is no original, an authenticatible copy will do.

---

[1] © 1999 Association of Certified Fraud Examiners

Bid-Rigging Schemes – The acceptance or payment of bribes or kickbacks in construction contracts. Bid-rigging schemes can be categorized based on the stage of bidding at which the fraudster exerts his influence. Bid-rigging schemes usually occur in the presolicitation phase, the solicitation phase, or the submission phase of the bidding process.

Billing Schemes – Type of asset misappropriation scheme which allows the perpetrator to misappropriate company funds without ever actually handling cash or checks while at work. There are three principal types of billing schemes: false invoicing via shell companies, false invoicing via nonaccomplice vendors, and personal purchases made with company funds.

Biological Theories – Biological theories maintain that criminal behavior is not the result of choice, that is, the calculation of benefits and potential losses, but rather is caused by the physical traits of those who commit crime.

***Brady* Material** – Exculpatory information possessed by the government. Refers to the 1963 decision by the U.S. Supreme Court in *Brady v. Maryland*, 373 U.S. 83. Under *Brady*, the prosecution must disclose all evidence requested by the defendant that is material to guilt or punishment, i.e., evidence that would tend to *exculpate* him or reduce his penalty. The government is expressly forbidden to conceal evidence that would call the charges into question.

Bribery – Includes official bribery, which refers to the corruption of a public official, and commercial bribery, which refers to the corruption of a private individual to gain a commercial or business advantage. The elements of official bribery vary by jurisdiction, but generally are (1) giving or receiving, (2) a thing of value, (3) to influence, (4) an official act.

Bustout – A planned bankruptcy. It can take many different forms. The basic approach is for an apparently legitimate business to order large quantities of goods on credit, then dispose of those goods through legitimate or illegitimate channels. The perpetrators then close shop, absconding with the proceeds, and leaving the suppliers unpaid.

Cash Larceny – The intentional taking away of an employer's cash (the term cash includes both currency and checks) without the consent and against the will of the employer.

Chain of Custody – Refers to (1) who has had possession of an object, and (2) what they have done with it. The chain of custody must be preserved or else the item cannot be used at trial.

Check Tampering – Type of fraudulent disbursement scheme in which the perpetrator physically prepares the fraudulent check. Usually, the perpetrator takes physical control of a check and makes it payable to himself through one of several methods. Most check tampering crimes fall into one of four categories: forged maker schemes, intercepted check schemes, concealed check schemes, and authorized maker schemes.

Chronemic Communication – Refers to the use of time in interpersonal relationships to convey meaning, attitudes, and desires. If the respondent is late in keeping an appointment, for example, this might convey a lack of interest in or avoidance of the interview.

Churning – Churning occurs when agents falsely tell customers that they can buy additional insurance for nothing by using built-up value in their current policies. In reality, the cost of the new policies frequently exceeds the value of the old ones.

Circumstantial Evidence – Evidence that tends to prove or disprove facts in issue indirectly, by inference. Many fraud cases are proved entirely by circumstantial evidence, or by a combination of circumstantial and direct evidence, but seldom by direct evidence alone. The most difficult element to prove in many fraud cases – fraudulent intent – is usually proved circumstantially, and necessarily so, because direct proof of the defendant's state of mind, absent a confession or the testimony of a co-conspirator, is impossible.

Civil Monetary Penalty Law (CMPL) – The Civil Monetary Penalty Law (42 U.S.C.§1320a-7a) was passed to impose administrative sanctions against providers who defraud any federally funded program by filing false claims or other improper billing practices. Any person (including an organization, agency, or other entity, but excluding a beneficiary) that presents or causes to be presented a claim for a medical or other item or service that the person knows or should know the claim is false or fraudulent is subject to a civil monetary penalty.

Common Law – Consists of the usages and customs of a society as interpreted by the judiciary; it often is referred to as "judge-made" law.

Computer Crime – Illegal act conducted either against the computer (such as data alteration) or crimes in which the computer is an integral part of the improper act.

Computer Fraud – Any defalcation or embezzlement accomplished by tampering with computer programs, data files, operations, equipment, or media, and resulting in losses sustained by the organization whose computer system was manipulated. The distinguishing characteristic of computer fraud is that access occurs with the intent to execute a fraudulent scheme.

Computer Fraud and Abuse Act – A statute enacted in 1984, Title 18 U.S. Code, Section 1030l makes certain computer-related activity a specific federal offense. In brief, Section 1030 punishes any intentional, unauthorized access to a "protected computer" for the purpose of: obtaining restricted data regarding national security; obtaining confidential financial information; using a computer which is intended for use by the U.S. government; committing a fraud; or damaging or destroying information contained in the computer.

Computer Hacking – Prior to the newspapers using the term *hacker* to describe a computer criminal, the term was used to define a computer enthusiast. The term is now associated with unauthorized computer activity. Hacking or phreaking is basically the breaking into computers and telecommunications systems by learning the vulnerabilities of various hardware and software; and using a computer to systematically "guess" the telephone number, user's system identification, and password.

Computer Viruses – A computer virus is a program that contains instruction codes to attack software. Viruses are hidden computer programs that use all the computer's resources, thereby shutting down the system or slowing it down significantly. Computer viruses range from the relatively harmless (displaying a message or greeting) to shutdowns of entire computer networks for extended periods.

Computer-Assisted Crime – Use of computers instead of other means to break the law.

Conflict of Interest – Occurs when an employee, manager, or executive has an undisclosed economic or personal interest in a transaction that adversely affects that person's employer. As with other corruption frauds, conflict schemes involve the exertion of an employee's influence to the detriment of his company. In bribery schemes, fraudsters are paid to exercise their influence on behalf of a third party. Conflict cases, instead, involve self-dealing by an employee.

Corporate Fraud – Corporate fraud is any fraud perpetrated by, for, or against a business corporation. Corporate frauds can be internally generated (perpetrated by agents, employees, and executives of a corporation, for or against it, or against others) and externally generated (by others against the corporation, i.e., suppliers, vendors, customers).

COSO Report – The Committee of Sponsoring Organizations (COSO) was formed to support the implementation of the Treadway Commission findings. In 1992, the committee issued *Internal Control–Integrated Framework*. This report was a collaborative effort of the American Accounting Association, the American Institute of CPAs, the Financial Executives Institute, the Institute of Internal Auditors, and the Institute of Management Accountants.

Counterclaims – A claim filed by a defendant against the plaintiff in a civil suit. Popularly known as a "countersuit."

Criteria-Based Statement Analysis – Analyzing the language used by the subject to assess its truthfulness.

Cross-Claim – An action or claim between co-parties, i.e., claims between two defendants or two plaintiffs.

Defalcation – The act of a defaulter; act of embezzling; failure to meet an obligation; misappropriation of trust funds or money held in any fiduciary capacity; failure to properly account for such funds. Commonly spoken of officers of corporations or public officials. (*Black's Law Dictionary*, 1990.)

Defamation – The four elements of defamation are (1) a false statement of fact, (2) tending to subject the person to whom it referred to ill will or disrepute, (3) published to one or more persons, and (4) made without privilege.

Defense – An assertion by a defendant in a criminal or civil suit that seeks to explain away guilt or civil liability for damages.

Demonstrative Evidence – A tangible item that illustrates some material proposition (e.g., a map, a chart, a summary). It differs from real evidence in that demonstrative evidence was not part of the underlying event: it was created specifically for the trial. Its purpose is to provide a visual aid for the jury.

Deposition – Sworn testimony given by a party or witness upon questioning by counsel for one of the parties before trial and outside of court, usually in a lawyer's office.

Direct Evidence – Includes testimony or other evidence that tends to prove or disprove a fact in issue directly, such as eyewitness testimony or a confession. See also **Circumstantial Evidence**.

Discovery – The formal process whereby the parties collect evidence and learn the details of the opposing case. Under federal rules, either party may take discovery regarding any matter, not privileged, that is relevant to the subject matter of the action, or that might lead to admissible evidence. The principal means of discovery are oral depositions, written interrogatories, and requests to produce documents.

Duty of Care – A corporate officer, director, or high-level employee, as well as other people in a fiduciary relationship, must conduct business affairs prudently with the skill and attention normally exercised by people in similar positions.

Duty of Loyalty – Requires that an employee/ agent act solely in the best interest of the employer/ principal, free of any self-dealing, conflicts of interest, or other abuse of the principal for personal advantage.

Economic Extortion – Economic extortion cases are the "Pay up or else . . ." corruption schemes; basically the flip side of bribery schemes. Instead of a vendor offering a payment to influence a decision, an employee demands that a vendor pay him in order to make a decision in that vendor's favor. If the vendor refuses to pay, he faces some harm such as a loss of business with the extorter's company.

Electronic Data Interchange – Electronic Data Interchange (EDI) is the exchange of electronic data between computers in which there is no human interaction.

Electronic Funds Transfer (EFT) – An electronic funds transfer (EFT) system is a network of operations designed to move instantaneously funds on deposit in savings and checking accounts and those funds obtained through overdraft and credit arrangements to another account or institution. (*Bank Administration Manual*, Bank Administration Institute.)

Embezzlement – The wrongful appropriation of money or property by a person to whom it has been lawfully entrusted. Embezzlement implicitly involves a breach of trust, although it is not necessary to show a fiduciary relationship between the parties.

Employee Polygraph Protection Act – Prohibits the use of polygraphs by most private employers unless the employer is engaged in an ongoing investigation involving economic loss or injury to the employer in the employer's business and has a reasonable suspicion that the employee is involved in the incident.

Encryption – An encryption system is comprised of a cryptographic function, which scrambles an electronic transmission, and an inverse decrypt function, which restores the transmission to its original state. Encryption hardware and software can be used to scramble any communication by utilizing a complex mathematical formula. The only way to unscramble an encrypted message is to provide the unique answer "key," thus unlocking the message.

Evidence – Anything perceivable by the five senses, and any proof such as testimony of witnesses, records, documents, facts, data, or tangible objects legally presented at trial to prove a contention and induce a belief in the minds of a jury.

Exclusionary Rule – This rule commands that where evidence has been obtained in violation of the search and seizure protections guaranteed by the U.S. Constitution, the illegally obtained evidence cannot be used at the trial of the defendant. Under this rule, evidence which is obtained by an unreasonable search and seizure is excluded from admissibility under the Fourth Amendment, and this rule has been held to be applicable to the States. "Good faith exception" to the exclusionary rule provides that evidence is not to be suppressed under such rule where that evidence was discovered by officers acting in good faith and in reasonable, though mistaken, belief that they were authorized to take those actions. (*Black's Law Dictionary*, 1990.)

Expert Witness –Rule 702 of the Federal Rules of Evidence states: "If scientific, technical, or other specialized knowledge will assist the trier of fact to understand the evidence or to determine a fact in issue, a witness qualified as an expert by knowledge, skill, experience, training, or education may testify thereto in the form of opinion or otherwise, if (1) the testimony is based upon sufficient facts or data, (2) the testimony is the product of reliable principles and methods, and (3) the witness has applied the principles and methods reliably to the facts of the case."

External Fraud Schemes – Fraud schemes that are committed by outside organizations, typically by individuals or groups of individuals against organizations.

Extortion – The obtaining of property from another with the other party's "consent" having been induced by wrongful use of actual or threatened force or fear. Fear might include the apprehension of possible economic damage or loss. A demand for a bribe or kickback also might constitute extortion.

Fair Credit Reporting Act – One of the primary statutes limiting the access to personal information is the federal Fair Credit Reporting Act (FCRA). This statute regulates the dissemination of consumer information to third parties by consumer reporting agencies. It prohibits the disclosure of any consumer credit report (the terms are defined in the statute) except in accordance with the Act. Its purpose is to regulate the activities and record keeping of mercantile credit, insurance, and employment investigation agencies and bureaus.

False Claims and Statements – Chapter 47 of Title 18, U.S. Code, contains a number of related provisions that punish false or fraudulent statements, orally or in writing, made to various federal agencies and departments. The principal statute is Section 1001 that prohibits such statements generally and overlaps with many of the more specific laws, such as Section 1014, that apply to false statements made on certain loan and credit applications.

False Imprisonment – Restraint by one person of the physical liberty of another without consent or legal justification.

False Pretenses – Illegally obtaining money, goods, or merchandise from another by fraud or misrepresentation. As a statutory crime, although defined in slightly different ways in the various jurisdictions, consists generally of these elements: (1) an intent to defraud (2) the use of false pretenses or representations regarding any existing facts, and (3) the accomplishment of the intended fraud by means of such false pretenses (*People v. Johnson*, 28 Mich. App. 10, 183 N.W.2d 813, 815, 816).

Fidelity Bond – A policy issued by many large insurance companies under which the insured entity is covered against losses caused by the dishonest or fraudulent acts of its employees.

Financial Statement Fraud – Fraud committed to falsify financial statements, usually committed by management, and normally involving overstating income or assets or understating liabilities or expenses.

Firewalls – Firewalls are advanced software programs which effectively "lock up" access to an Internet sight or e-mail transmission. Firewalls are designed to control the interface between a network and the Internet. This technology surveys incoming and outgoing transmissions between the network and the Internet, stopping any questionable transmission attempt to access a sensitive area.

Foreign Corrupt Practices Act – The provisions of the FCPA are found in Title 15, U.S. Code, §78m. The FCPA amended the 1934 Act to prohibit certain publicly held companies from making corrupt payments to foreign officials or political organizations. Other amendments to the Act make it illegal for any U.S. citizen to make such payments.

Forensic – Of or relating to the courts.

Fraud – Any intentional or deliberate act to deprive another of property or money by guile, deception or other unfair means.

Fraud Examination – A methodology for resolving fraud allegations from inception to disposition. More specifically, fraud examination involves obtaining evidence and taking statements, writing reports, testifying to findings, and assisting in the detection and prevention of fraud.

Fraud Theory Approach – The fraud theory approach begins with the assumption, based on the known facts, of what might have occurred. Then that assumption is tested to determine whether it is provable. The fraud theory approach involves the following steps, in the order of their occurrence: (1) analyze available data; (2) create a hypothesis; (3) test the hypothesis; (4) refine and amend the hypothesis.

Fraudulent Disbursement Schemes – Type of occupational fraud whereby an employee makes a distribution of company funds for a dishonest purpose. Examples of fraudulent disbursements include forging company checks, the submission of false invoices, doctoring timecards, and so forth.

Ghost Employee – Refers to someone on the payroll who does not actually work for the victim company. Through the falsification of personnel or payroll records a fraudster causes paychecks to be generated to a ghost. The fraudster or an accomplice then converts these paychecks. The ghost employee may be a fictitious person or a real individual who simply does not work for the victim employer. When the ghost is a real person, it is often a friend or relative of the perpetrator.

Grand Jury – Consists of 16 to 23 people sworn as jurors who meet in secret deliberation usually in biweekly or monthly sessions to hear witnesses and other evidence presented by prosecutors and to vote on indictments. An indictment or *true bill* must be concurred in by at least 12 jurors voting without the prosecutor present.

Horizontal Analysis – A technique for analyzing the percentage change in individual financial statement items from one year to the next. The first period in the analysis is considered the base, and the changes to subsequent periods are computed as a percentage of the base period.

Illegal Gratuities – Similar to bribery schemes, except there is not necessarily an intent to influence a particular business decision before the fact. In the typical illegal gratuities scenario, a decision is made which happens to benefit a certain person or company. The party who benefited from the decision then gives a gift to the person who made the decision. The gift could be anything of value. An illegal gratuity does not require proof of intent to influence.

Indictment – In the federal system, all offenses punishable by death must be charged by indictment; all felonies (generally crimes punishable by imprisonment for a year or more) must be prosecuted by indictment, unless the defendant waives the requirement, in which case the prosecution may proceed by the filing of an *Information*.

Information – A charge signed only by the prosecutor without the involvement of the grand jury. See also **Indictment**.

Insider Trading – Consists of using nonpublic information relating to market securities trades.

Interrogatories – Questions that are submitted to an opposing party in a lawsuit. Interrogatories cannot be given to anyone other than a party to a suit. Questions are submitted to the witness in writing. If no objection is given, then the party must answer the question in writing. All answers must be sworn to under oath.

Interview – A question-and-answer session designed to elicit information. It differs from an ordinary conversation in that the interview is structured, not free-form, and is designed for a purpose. An interview might consist of only one question or a series of questions.

Jencks Act – The Jencks Act, 18 U.S.C. §3500, permits the defendant to obtain, prior to cross-examination, a government witness' prior statements (or portions thereof) that relate to the subject matter of his testimony on direct examination. However, the statute also protects statements from discovery until after the direct examination has been completed.

Jurisdiction – Authority of a court to hear a particular type of case. A probate court, for instance, only has jurisdiction to hear cases related to wills and other probate matters. Lower trial courts (such as a justice of the peace court) may only have jurisdiction to hear matters under a certain dollar amount, e.g., cases with less than $5,000 in controversy.

Kickbacks – In the commercial sense, refers to the giving or receiving anything of value to influence a business decision without the employer's knowledge and consent.

Kinesic Interview – Type of interview methodology that is different than traditional interview methods, because the interviewer is not necessarily looking for a confession from the interview subject. Instead of searching for information from the subject, the interviewer is attempting to assess whether the subject is telling the truth. In the book *The Kinesic Interview Technique*, authors Frederick C. Link and D. Glen Foster define the kinesic interview technique as "[An interview technique] used for gaining information from an individual who is not willingly or intentionally disclosing it."

Kinetic Communication – Involves the use of body movement to convey meaning. For example, a person who feels shame normally will drop the eyes to avoid the glance of another. This is not only to avoid seeing disapproval, but to conceal personal shame and confusion.

Kiting – The wrongful practice of taking advantage of the float, the time that elapses between the deposit of a check in one bank and its collection at another. Method of drawing checks by which the drawer uses funds which are not his by drawing checks against deposits which have not yet cleared through the banks. Kiting consists of writing checks against a bank account where funds are insufficient to cover them, hoping that before they are presented the necessary funds will be deposited. (*Black's Law Dictionary*, 1990.)

Land Flip – Practice of buying and selling real estate very quickly, often several times a day or at least within a few months. With each sale the price is increased. The sales often are transacted between related parties or with shell corporations. Their sole purpose is to increase the selling price. Ultimately, it becomes insupportable.

Larceny – The wrongful taking of money or property of another with the intent to convert or to deprive the owner of its possession and use.

Libel – Form of defamation whereby the offending material is communicated by writing or pictures as opposed to purely oral means.

Mail Fraud – The federal mail fraud statute is Title 18, U.S. Code, §1341. The gist of the offense is the use of the mails as an integral part of a scheme to defraud. The mailing does not itself need to contain the false and fraudulent representations, as long as it is an integral part of the scheme. What is integral or incidental depends on the facts of each case; generally a mailing that helps advance the scheme in any significant way will be considered sufficient.

Mediation – Process whereby an impartial third-person assists the parties in reaching a resolution of the dispute. The mediator does not decide who should win, but instead works with the parties to reach a mutually agreeable settlement.

***Miranda* Rights** – Refers to the Supreme Court ruling in the landmark case of *Miranda v. Arizona*, 348 U.S. 436 (1966), that the police must give the following warnings before interrogating any suspect held in custody that (1) the suspect has the right to remain silent; (2) any statements can be used against him at trial; (3) the suspect has a right to the assistance of an attorney; and (4) an attorney will be appointed to represent the suspect if he cannot afford to retain one.

Misapplication – Wrongful taking or conversion of another's property for the benefit of someone else.

Misappropriation – The unauthorized, improper, or unlawful use of funds or other property for purpose other than that for which intended.

Misrepresentation of Material Facts – The deliberate making of false statements to induce the intended victim to part with money or property. The elements normally include (1) a material false statement; (2) knowledge of its falsity; (3) reliance on the false statement by the victim; and (4) damages suffered.

Money Laundering – The disguising of the existence, nature, source, ownership, location, and disposition of property derived from criminal activity. The "washing" of money includes all forms of illegal activities. In most instances the goal is to conduct transactions in cash (currency) in such a way as to conceal the true nature of transactions.

Multi-Level Marketing (MLM) – Use of individual sellers and a graduated payment scale to move products. Illegal MLMs use the product as a front while basing their return on new people recruited into the plan.

Net Worth – The amount by which assets exceed liabilities.

Noncompetition Agreement – An agreement whereby an employee agrees not to work for competing companies within a certain period of time after leaving.

Nondisclosure Agreement – A written agreement which provides that all proprietary, confidential, or trade secret information learned by the party in the course of business dealings must be kept confidential and must not be disclosed to any third-parties.

Norming – Sometimes referred to as calibrating, norming is the process of observing behavior before critical questions are asked, as opposed to doing so during questioning. People with truthful attitudes will answer questions one way; those with untruthful attitudes generally will answer them differently.

Occupational Fraud and Abuse – The use of one's occupation for personal enrichment through the deliberate misuse or misapplication of the employing organization's resources or assets. Simply stated, occupational frauds are those in which an employee, manager, officer, or owner of an organization commits fraud to the detriment of that organization. The three major types of occupational fraud are Corruption, Asset Misappropriation, and Fraudulent Statements (which include financial statement schemes).

Off-Book Frauds – Involves vendor and vendor employees engaging in bribes, scams, kickbacks, conflicts of interest, bribery, and corruption. Detected by means of tips or complaints from sources either inside or outside the company.

On-Book Frauds – Involves employees manipulating accounting records. Detected by means of basic audit tests in high-risk areas using original source documents.

Oversight Committee – An oversight committee should be established to review uniformity in decision making. Further, it should act as a tribunal for the presentation of additional information to change or assist management in making appropriate decisions regarding fraud investigations.

Paralinguistic Communication – Involves the use of volume, pitch, and voice quality to convey meaning. One of the basic differences between written and verbal communication is that oral speech gives the full range of nonverbal accompaniment. For example, a "no" answer might not really mean no; it depends on the way in which the "no" is said.

Parol Evidence – Oral or verbal evidence; that which is given by word of mouth; the ordinary kind of evidence given by witnesses in court. (*Black's Law Dictionary*, 1990.)

Parol Evidence Rule – This evidence rule seeks to preserve integrity of written agreements by refusing to permit contracting parties to attempt to alter import of their contract through use of contemporaneous oral declarations. (*Black's Law Dictionary*, 1990.)

Ponzi Scheme – The term *Ponzi* refers to illegal operations which use financial instruments of some sort to extract money from victims; there are few or no actual investments being made, just funds passing up a ladder.

Privacy Act of 1974 – Restricts information about individuals, both employees and non-employees, that might be gathered by *government agencies*. This information might include a person's education, finances, medical history, criminal history, employment history, and identifying information (fingerprint, voice print, or photograph). The employee might have access to the information unless it is investigatory material compiled for law enforcement purposes, statistical records, or material compiled solely for determining suitability, eligibility, or qualification for federal service or promotion.

Probable Cause – Reasonable cause; having more evidence for than against. A reasonable ground for belief in certain alleged facts. A set of probabilities grounded in the factual and practical considerations which govern the decisions of reasonable and prudent persons and is more than mere suspicion but less than the quantum of evidence required for conviction. (*Black's Law Dictionary*, 1990.)

Proxemic Communication – Use of interpersonal space to convey meaning. The relationship between the interviewer and respondent is both a cause and effect of proxemic behavior. If the distance between the interviewer and the respondent is greater, there is more of a tendency for them to watch each other's eyes for clues to meaning.

Psychological Theories – Refers to theories of behavior rooted in psychology and which are based on the view that criminal behavior is the product of mental processes.

Pyramid Scheme – A scheme in which a buyer or participant is promised a payment for each additional buyer or participant recruited by that person.

Qui Tam Suit – A *qui tam* suit is one in which a private individual sues on behalf of the government to recover damages for criminal or fraudulent actions committed against the government. It is a civil not a criminal suit. Most qui tam actions are brought under the False Claims Act, 31 USC §3729 et seq.

Racketeer Influenced and Corrupt Organizations Act (RICO) – Title 18, U.S. Code, §1961, et. seq. The statute outlaws the investment of ill-gotten gains in another business enterprise; the acquisition of an interest in an enterprise through certain illegal acts; and the conduct of the affairs of an enterprise through such acts. Criminal penalties include stiff fines and prison terms as well as the forfeiture of all illegal proceeds or interests. Civil remedies include treble damages, attorney fees, dissolution of the offending enterprise, and other penalties.

Ratio Analysis – A means of measuring the relationship between two different financial statement amounts. The relationship and comparison are the keys to the analysis.

Real Evidence – Refers to physical objects which may be introduced as evidence at a legal proceeding. A canceled check, an invoice, a ledger, letters and documents are real evidence, but the term includes any physical evidence.

Relevant Evidence – Rule 401 of the Federal Rules of Evidence defines *relevant evidence* as evidence "having any tendency to make the existence of any fact that is of consequence to determination of the action more probable or less probable than it would be without the evidence." In other words, relevant evidence is evidence that tends to prove or disprove a fact in issue.

Routine Activities Theory – A variation of classical theory, this theory holds that both the motivation to commit crime and the supply of offenders is constant. There always will be a certain number of people motivated by greed, lust, and other forces inclining toward lawbreaking.

Search Warrants – Issued by a judge upon presentation of probable cause to believe the records are being used or have been used in the commission of a crime. An affidavit usually is used to support the request for the search warrant. The affidavit must describe in detail the reason(s) the warrant is requested, along with the place the evidence is thought to be kept. Courts cannot issue search warrants without sufficient cause; the Fourth Amendment to the Constitution protects individuals against unreasonable searches and seizures.

Sentencing Guidelines – The Sentencing Reform Act of 1984 provided for the development of guidelines for the sentencing of individual and organizational offenders. The individual guidelines became effective in 1987, and the guidelines for organizations in 1991.

Shell Companies – Fictitious business entities created for the sole purpose of committing fraud. They may be nothing more than a fabricated name and a post office box that an employee uses to collect disbursements from false billings.

Skimming – Removal of cash from a victim entity prior to its entry in an accounting system. Employees who skim from their companies steal sales or receivables before they are recorded in the company books. Skimming schemes are known as "off-book" frauds, meaning money is stolen before it is recorded in the victim organization's accounts.

Sliding – Sliding is the term used for including additional coverages in the insurance policy without the knowledge of the insured. The extra charges are hidden in the total premium and since the insured is unaware of the coverage, few claims are ever filed. For example, motor club memberships, accidental death, and travel accident coverages can usually be slipped into the policy without the knowledge of the insured.

Social Control Theory – Travis Hirschi, in his 1969 book, *Causes of Delinquency*, first articulated the *social control theory*. Essentially, control theory argues that the institutions of the social system train and press those with whom they are in contact into patterns of conformity. The theory rests on the thesis that to the extent a person fails to become attached to the variety of control agencies of the society, his/ her chances of violating the law are increased.

Social Learning Theories – These theories hold that criminal behavior is a function of the way people absorb information, viewpoints, and motivations from others, most notably from those to whom they are close, such as members of their peer group. Social learning theorists believe that all people have the potential to commit crime if they are exposed to certain kinds of circumstances.

Social Process Theories – These theories hold that criminality is a function of individual socialization and the social-psychological interactions people have with the various organizations, institutions, and processes of society. Though they differ in many respects, the various social process theories all share one basic concept: all people regardless of their race, class, or gender, have the potential to become delinquents or criminals.

Social Structure Theories – Theories of criminology that concentrate on the kinds of societies that generate particular levels of crime, for example, why is crime so low in Japan and so high in the United States? Such theorists argue that people living in equivalent social environments seem to behave in a similar, predictable fashion.

Subpoena Duces Tecum – A legal order requiring the production of documents.

Suspicious Activity Reports – Effective April 1, 1996, the Office of the Comptroller of the Currency (OCC) requires national banks to submit a Suspicious Activity Report (SAR) under certain circumstances (12 C.F.R. §21.11, as amended). Reports are required if there is a known or suspected criminal violation committed against the bank or involving a transaction conducted through the bank.

Tax Fraud – "... the actual intentional wrongdoing, and the intent required ... to evade a tax believed to be owing. Fraud implies bad faith, intentional wrongdoing, and a sinister motive. It is never imputed or presumed and the courts will not sustain findings of fraud upon circumstances which at most create only suspicion. 14 Mertens, *Law of Federal Income Taxation*, sec. 55.21, page 64, (1991 Rev); *Ross Glove Co. v. Commissioner*, 60 TC 569 (1973).

Telemarketing Fraud – Used to refer to fraud schemes which are perpetrated over the telephone; most often consists of calls by the telemarketer to the victim to deceive the victim into purchasing goods or services.

Trade Secret – Includes secret formulas and processes, but also any other proprietary information, such as customer and price lists, sales figures, business plans, or any other confidential information that has a value to the business and would be potentially harmful if disclosed.

Treadway Commission – The National Commission on Fraudulent Financial Reporting (commonly known as the Treadway Commission) was established in 1987 with the purpose of defining the responsibility of the auditor in preventing and detecting fraud. The commission was formed by the major professional auditing organizations – the American Institute of Certified Public Accountants, the Institute of Internal Auditors, and the National Association of Accountants.

Trespass – The unauthorized, intentional or negligent entry upon the property of others. A claim of trespass might arise from a search of an employee's locker. It is particularly applicable to surveillance at an employee's home.

Twisting – Twisting is the replacement, usually by high pressure sales techniques, of existing policies for new ones. The primary reason, of course, is for the agent to profit since first year sales commissions are much higher than commissions for existing policies.

Uniform Commercial Code Filings – In order to obtain a perfected security interest in personal property, a lender must file a Uniform Commercial Code (UCC) statement with the Secretary of State or the county. Banks, finance companies and other lenders will generate records or recorded filings of financial transactions conducted with individuals and businesses, such as purchases of household furniture, appliances, boats and yachts, automobiles, aircraft, and business equipment.

Uniform Crime Reports – The Federal Bureau of Investigation (FBI) compiles statistics on the extent of crime in the United States in a document called the Uniform Crime Report (UCR). The report is put together on the basis of information voluntarily submitted by more than 15,000 law enforcement departments. This includes virtually every significant public policing agency in the country.

Venue – The geographical area covered by the court. A trial court in Dallas County, Texas, for example, can only hear cases which have some connection with either parties or events that occurred in that county. Venue is technically an element of the court's jurisdiction.

Vertical Analysis – A technique for analyzing the relationships between the items on an income statement, balance sheet, or statement of cash flows by expressing components as percentages.

Whistleblower – Employees who report illegal or unethical conduct of their employers. Federal law and many state laws provide, in some instances, protection to employees who report improper or illegal acts to government authorities. Most of these laws protect the employee from any adverse employment action or retaliatory action from the employer.

Wire Fraud – The federal wire fraud statute is Title 18, U.S. Code, §1343. It prohibits transmission "by means of wire, radio, or television communication in interstate or foreign commerce, any writings, signs, signals, pictures, or sounds for the purpose of executing such scheme or artifice." The wire fraud statute often is used in tandem with mail fraud counts in federal prosecutions. Unlike mail fraud, however, the wire fraud statute requires an interstate or foreign communication for a violation.

Yellow Book Standards – Standards for audits of government organizations, programs, activities, and functions, and of government assistance received by contractors, nonprofit organizations, and other non-government organizations developed by the Comptroller General of the United States, General Accounting Office (GAO). These standards are by and large taken from generally accepted accounting principles. However, *Government Auditing Standards* also known as the *Yellow Book*, go beyond the AICPA standards. Generally accepted government auditing standards (GAGAS) are to be followed by auditors and audit organizations when required by law, regulation, agreement, contract, or policy.

Index

A

B

C

E

G

M

O

P

R

Frequent Frauds Found in Governments and Not-For-Profits

By Lynda Dennis, Ph.D., CPA, CGFO

Solutions

The AICPA offers a free, daily, e-mailed newsletter covering the day's top business and financial articles as well as video content, research and analysis concerning CPAs and those who work with the accounting profession. Visit the CPA Letter Daily news box on the www.aicpa.org home page to sign up. You can opt out at any time, and only the AICPA can use your e-mail address or personal information.

Have a technical accounting or auditing question? So did 23,000 other professionals who contacted the AICPA's accounting and auditing Technical Hotline last year. The objectives of the hotline are to enhance members' knowledge and application of professional judgment by providing free, prompt, high-quality technical assistance by phone concerning issues related to: accounting principles and financial reporting; auditing, attestation, compilation and review standards. The team extends this technical assistance to representatives of governmental units. The hotline can be reached at 1-877-242-7212.

SOLUTIONS

CHAPTER 1

Suggested Solutions to Case 1

1. By misstating the interim quarterly information, the county appeared to be in compliance with its bond covenants when in fact it was not. In this case, management override occurred in two situations. The first was when Robert asked the public works superintendent to process a purchase order without issuing it. In the second situation of management override, Robert adjusted the tax collections using journal entries. Both of these situations occurred because Robert was in a position to pressure employees and exercise management override over recorded amounts through journal entries. In this case, no one appears to review journal entries made by the finance director. Even if the county manager were reviewing journal entries made by the finance director, she may not have understood them. It is also likely she might have involved herself in the fraud as she was under pressure from the county commission and felt her job was in jeopardy.
2. The following preliminary procedures might have detected this situation:
   - Review of the interim financial statements (may have indicated a decline in tax collections or a downward trend in the collection ratio).
   - Inquiries of the county manager as well as other managers (for example, public works superintendent) and administrative staff.
   - Reviewing bond covenants for potential pressure on management (management pressure or incentive to meet the covenants).
   - Review of the controls over journal entries (potential for management override by the finance director).
3. Other procedures that might have detected this situation would include the following:
   - Review of quarterly information (including tracing amounts to reports, documentation, and so on) sent to bond oversight agencies.
   - Confirmation of taxes collected and remitted to cities in the county and the related remission dates.
   - Analytical review of tax collections by month (ratio collected, comparison with prior years, and the like).
   - Review of journal entries.
4. The auditor should communicate this situation to both the county manager and those charged with governance (for example, the county commission audit committee) as it was perpetrated by management (the finance director). Additionally, the auditor would need to consider whether to report this to other third parties. The auditor would re-evaluate any previously planned reliance on internal controls (especially any reliance placed on the finance director function, purchasing, and cash receipts) and whether the planned procedures need to be expanded in light of this situation.

Solutions to Knowledge Check Questions

1.

a. Incorrect. Billing schemes are an area where management may override existing controls.
b. Incorrect. Journal entries are an area where management may override existing controls.
c. Incorrect. Estimates are an area where management may override existing controls.
d. Correct. Price fixing between two vendors is not something an entity controls; therefore, management cannot override any of the entity's controls in this circumstance.

2.

a. Correct. Balsa Wood County is a full service, medium-sized county.
b. Incorrect. The county provides a number of services to the cities within its boundaries through various interlocal agreements.
c. Incorrect. Balsa Wood grew slowly until the mid-1950s.
d. Incorrect. Balsa Wood issued bonds to fund road improvements and to build a minor league baseball stadium.

3.

a. Correct. The county remits collections, net of a two percent administrative charge, to the cities bi-weekly during peak collection periods (such as the first six months after taxes are levied) and monthly during non-peak collection periods.
b. Incorrect. All cities use the county tax assessor and collector to assess and collect their municipal taxes.
c. Incorrect. Growth in the state virtually halted in the late 1970s.
d. Incorrect. The county has had to increase tax rates in recent years.

4.

a. Correct. The recently built stadium facility is used mainly for area concerts and high school sporting events.
b. Incorrect. The decision to build the baseball stadium was made prior to employing the current county manager.
c. Incorrect. The county lost its bid for a minor league baseball expansion team.
d. Incorrect. The county is not on the verge of bankruptcy and even if it were, it would file for bankruptcy under Chapter 9.

5.

a. Incorrect. The county and the trustee for the bonds entered into a number of covenants with respect to the general obligation bonds.
b. Correct. Should any of the covenants related to the general obligation bonds be violated, the bonds may be called by the trustee.
c. Incorrect. The county is required to have audited financial statements.
d. Incorrect. The finance director manipulated property tax collections in the current year to meet bond covenants.

CHAPTER 2

Suggested Solutions to Case 2

1. Elements of the fraud triangle present include the following:
   - There is pressure on management to provide the planned programs and services with fewer financial resources.
   - Opportunity exists at the branch locations due to limited staff and oversight (DHHS procedures actually increase the potential for fraud at branch locations).
   - Management believes strongly in their mission which could lead to rationalization of fraudulent transactions.
   - Branch personnel are not paid commensurate with their needs or expectations.
2. Additional procedures the CFO could have taken include the following:
   - Review of total files processed by each branch location and by which branch personnel.
   - Inquiry of branch personnel as to changes in life styles of branch employees.
   - Sampling a few files from each branch to determine validity of applicant name, address, and income level.
   - Confirmation with DHHS of total amounts sent to each branch by applicant.
   - Comparison of DHHS checks received to applicant files and to branch deposits.
3. Missing or inadequate internal controls include the following:
   - Lacking controls at branch locations.
   - Limited supervision of branch personnel in a position to perpetrate fraud due to limited or missing controls.
   - Over-reliance by branch management on branch support staff.
   - Lack of central oversight or control of branch activities and transactions.
4. Preliminary audit procedures might include the following:
   - Assessment of branch locations for potential material fraud.
   - Review of controls at selected branch locations.
   - Inquiry of selected branch personnel at all levels regarding the potential for fraud.
   - Review of grant provisions and assessment of related controls over grant transactions.

   Other audit procedures might include the following:

   - Review of files processed by each branch location.
   - Sampling selected files from each branch to determine validity of applicant name, address, and income level.
   - Confirmation with DHHS of total amounts sent to each branch by applicant.
   - Comparison of DHHS checks received to applicant files and to branch deposits.

Solutions to Knowledge Check Questions

1.

   a. Incorrect. Healthy Families receives 40 percent of operating revenues from program fees.
   b. Correct. Healthy Families is a United Way agency and as such receives approximately $300,000 each year.
   c. Incorrect. Healthy Families operates in a five-county area.
   d. Incorrect. Healthy Families receives 75 percent of its funds from program fees and membership dues.

2.

a. Incorrect. Each branch is staffed with at least one program coordinator and a full or part-time office manager.
b. Incorrect. Healthy Families has 25 branch locations offering various program services.
c. Correct. Branch operations range from providing minimal services off-site to providing a full range of services both on and off-site.
d. Incorrect. Branch operations are subject to limited oversight by administrative office executive leadership.

3.

a. Correct. The board formally adopted a written personnel policy two years ago that included hiring and firing guidelines for branch managers.
b. Incorrect. Each branch manager hires and fires all personnel needed to operate the branch.
c. Incorrect. The board formally adopted a written personnel policy two years ago.
d. Incorrect. All branch personnel are directly involved in the annual fundraising appeal.

4.

a. Incorrect. Administrative office personnel and branch managers are compensated commensurate with prevailing market rates for similar work.
b. Correct. No formal compensation system exists at any level of the organization as the local economic circumstances of the various branch office locations dictate branch salaries.
c. Incorrect. The annual fundraising appeal is conducted each February.
d. Incorrect. Healthy Families has very little grant funding and annually conducts a fundraising appeal.

5.

a. Incorrect. Healthy Families employs a full-time development director.
b. Correct. For the past 25 years, Healthy Families has employed a professional development director.
c. Incorrect. To date, Healthy Families has had very little grant activity because staff does not want to be limited by grant provisions and procedures.
d. Incorrect. The current development director was hired from a large not-for-profit.

CHAPTER 3

Suggested Solutions to Case 3

1. As is the case in small organizations, a lack of controls may exist due to limited personnel or personnel with limited training. Additionally, in many small governmental organizations, management (such as, department heads, managers, and so on) may be in a position to influence staff and elected officials which could lead to management override in the areas discussed. Certain governmental functions, such as public safety, are hierarchical in nature which may also represent a potential fraud risk.
2. Helpful procedures could have included the following:
   - Analytical procedures related to payroll expenses and compliance (assuming properly designed controls are in place) and substantive tests of details.

- Ratio analyses of departmental payroll and payroll related expenses might have indicated a high ratio of overtime in the affected departments. A review of W-2 amounts to base salaries would indicate any employees for which overtime was a large component of their annual compensation.
- Compliance tests related to controls, if any, related to overtime might have detected the situations outlined in this case. Typical compliance procedures often only look to see overtime was approved when they might need to also determine the legitimacy of the overtime.

3. Controls related to the legitimacy of overtime should be in place. For example, controls should be in place to assure (*a*) overtime is actually worked and (*b*) it was for legitimate public purposes. In the case of 24-hour personnel, controls related to whether work was actually performed or necessary are often missing or ineffective.
4. The auditor might suggest increasing controls related to overtime in order to assure its legitimacy and public purpose. Additionally, the auditor might suggest the new Town Manager look into industry-type standards related to salaries, overtime, shift length, and so on. Some governmental organizations have in place a "one dollar more" policy ensuring management is paid at least "one dollar more" than any one they supervise. Such a policy ensures total compensation is reviewed periodically (usually annually) and appropriate actions are taken to prevent or deter overtime abuses.
5. This case presents a very sensitive area for both management and external auditors. Public safety functions are usually considered first in the budget process due to public perceptions, and the like. Although the situations outlined in this case may or may not represent financial statement fraud, they do appear to be at least abuse.

Solutions to Knowledge Check Questions

1.

a. Incorrect. The police department does allow employees to work overtime.
b. Incorrect. Billy wishes to take his future wife on a nice honeymoon but does not know how he will have the money for it.
c. Correct. There appears to be either fraud or abuse occurring with respect to overtime in the police department.
d. Incorrect. The town of Sea Side has a full-time police department.

2.

a. Incorrect. A lot of the town's employees earned well over their base pay.
b. Incorrect. One of the first things the new town manager requested was a copy of the budget for the last three years.
c. Correct. When factoring in overtime, a lot of the town employees made more money than their department head.
d. Incorrect. Sea Side has employees that are and are not exempt from federal requirements to pay overtime.

3.

a. Incorrect. The town of Sea Side is a small town.
b. Correct. The finance director describes the town as a small shop where getting good controls and procedures in place has been a little tough.
c. Incorrect. The finance director is looking forward to working for the new town manager who knows something about accounting and finance.
d. Incorrect. No information in the case is given regarding the finance director's satisfaction with her job.

4.

a. Incorrect. Prior to joining the town of Sea Side the town manager worked for a medium-sized city.
b. Correct. The town council hired the new town manager for his financial expertise and economic development experience.
c. Incorrect. The case does not mention that the finance director is a CGMA.
d. Incorrect. The town manager is not a practicing CPA.

Chapter 4

Suggested Solutions to Case 4

1. The actions of the staff of Seniors Forever, however well intentioned, represent fraud resulting from management override. They have fraudulently represented grant transactions.
2. Preliminary procedures that might have detected this situation include the following:
   - Ratio analysis of direct and administrative costs to total costs
   - Preliminary inquiries of program directors
   - Consideration of external environment (that is, reduced state funding) in light of the organization and the fraud triangle
3. Other audit procedures that might have detected this situation include the following:
   - Compliance tests of controls (assuming controls are properly designed and in place)
   - Substantive tests of details
   - Tests of program disbursements

Solutions to Knowledge Check Questions

1.

a. Correct. The governor is proposing a massive state-wide agency reorganization that could affect Seniors Forever.
b. Incorrect. The biggest state-funded program is the Nutrition First program which allows Seniors Forever to provide hot meals to seniors five days a week.
c. Incorrect. The largest state-funded program is not the Keep on Truckin' program.
d. Incorrect. Most of the funding for Senior Forever comes from state grants.

2.

a. Incorrect. The Keep on Truckin' program is funded primarily with three state grants.
b. Correct. The second biggest state-funded program is in the second of a five-year contract and gives Seniors Forever $500,000 each year to subsidize adult day care for seniors in Tangerine County.
c. Incorrect. Seniors Forever has a number of grants to fund its multiple programs.
d. Incorrect. One grant funding the Keep on Truckin' program is a three-year "bus grant" that provides $100,000 annually to subsidize bus passes for seniors in Tangerine County.

CHAPTER 5

Suggested Solutions to Case 5

1. This case represents a potential fraud risk resulting from management override. In this case, top management sanctions "bending the rules" that sets the tone for the entire organization. Additionally, onerous policies and procedures (for example, requiring quotes or bids for relatively small thresholds) may encourage management to override controls for expediency as was done in this case.
2. In this case, the city commission has placed pressure on the city manager to conduct its citizen survey within a short window of time.
3. A review of commission meeting minutes might bring pressure type situations to light which the auditor may or may not consider in the planning or subsequent stages of the engagement. Preliminary inquiries of city staff, especially accounts payable personnel or the finance director, might also detect this situation.
4. Substantive tests of details or compliance tests related to controls over purchasing and cash disbursements (assuming controls are properly designed and in place) might detect this situation. Utilizing technology, the auditor could have a report created for all disbursements and purchase orders that are close to established thresholds. Any items close to threshold amounts could be reviewed for possible manipulation (that is, splitting purchases) or management override.
5. Responses to this question will vary based on the experiences and attitudes of the participants.

Solutions to Knowledge Check Questions

1.

a. Correct. Commission members approved $25,000 from the commission contingency fund be used for a citizen survey.
b. Incorrect. Commission members told the city manager to make the citizen survey a priority.
c. Incorrect. The city utilizes a contingency fund.
d. Incorrect. Funding the citizen survey from the contingency fund was approved by all commission members.

2.

a. Correct. A $25,000 purchase order for a citizen survey was originated by the budget director and approved by the city manager.
b. Incorrect. A $24,900 purchase order for a citizen survey was not originated by the budget director and approved by the city manager.
c. Incorrect. Formal bids were not received on the citizen survey in accordance with the city's purchasing policy.
d. Incorrect. The city undergoes a tri-annual citizen survey.

CHAPTER 6

Suggested Solutions to Case 6

1. The risk of material financial statement misstatement is present in this case because the organization is involved in fundraising for both capital and operating needs. Specific fraud risks relate to revenue recognition including propriety and classification of pledges as well as the collectability of such amounts.
2. Management has the incentive to misstate capital campaign contributions in order to obtain external financing. They may rationalize this because they believe very strongly in the organization's mission and the need for the facilities in the community. The short time frame given by the board of directors to raise the funds puts pressure on management that might result in management feeling pressured to misrepresent financial statement amounts. Additionally, the bonus structure approved by the Board provides all staff involved in fund raising efforts an incentive to misstate capital campaign contributions. The promise of additional program funding in the next year for those exceeding their goal might also provide the rationalization management needs to fraudulently represent capital fund raising efforts. The development director also has the opportunity to misstate contributions as there appear to be few controls over the capital fund raising process. This situation persists, in part, because the CFO appears to have little time for oversight because he is also involved in the fund raising efforts.
3. Because this is the organization's first capital campaign, the auditor will not be able to compare this year's results with prior efforts. However, results could be compared to industry benchmarks obtained from national (for example, BBB Wise Giving Alliance, and so on) or local organizations. Discussions with client personnel could also help bring light to the matter.
4. Because this is the organization's first capital campaign, the auditor might consider confirming a large number of small and large capital and operating campaign contributions directly with donors. For those pledges not confirmed, if felt necessary, the auditor could match donor names and addresses to the phone book, and the like. In some cases, the addresses of donors could be matched to community data, employee addresses, prior giving history, and so on. The auditor could also perform analytical and substantive testing on the pledges collected to date and a low percentage could bring attention to the validity of the pledges.
5. Responses to this question will vary based on the experience and attitudes of participants.

Solution to Knowledge Check Questions

1.

   a. Incorrect. To fund construction, the Board authorized the CEO to solicit proposals from area banks for construction and permanent financing.
   b. Incorrect. We Care is a 501(c)(3).
   c. Correct. At a recent meeting, the board of directors approved plans to expand the existing shelter to house an additional 20 residents and to construct a new shelter in the southern portion of the county.
   d. Incorrect. The development director prepares the capital campaign plan.

CHAPTER 7

Suggested Solutions to Case 7

1. Physical inspection of selected assets, typically those subject to misappropriation and personal use, could be performed. Additionally, inquiries could be made of city personnel regarding their knowledge of any personal use of city owned assets.
2. Responses to this question will vary based on the experience and attitudes of the participants. However, participants should discuss that the fraud and abuse outlined in this case can be very sensitive because it appears to involve elected officials as well as management. Participants should also discuss how reporting of the situation would depend on the quantitative and qualitative aspect of the fraud and abuse.

Solutions to Knowledge Check Questions

1.

a. Incorrect. River City does have formal written capital asset policies.
b. Correct. River City is a medium-sized city with operations centrally located at the City Hall complex as well as several off-site locations.
c. Incorrect. Off-site operations include two city parks, three fire stations, two police substations, a city-owned and operated garage, and the water and sewer plant.
d. Incorrect. River City has engaged a new audit firm.

2.

a. Incorrect. For buildings, the capitalization threshold is $25,000.
b. Correct. The city's capitalization threshold is $5,000 for vehicles, furniture and fixtures, and equipment.
c. Incorrect. For infrastructure assets the capitalization threshold is $50,000.
d. Incorrect. Assets not subject to the city's capitalization policy are not required to be tagged.

3.

a. Correct. The IT department maintains all computer and computer-related equipment.
b. Incorrect. All computer and computer-related equipment is identified and tracked.
c. Incorrect. Asset tags are pre-numbered and required to be used sequentially.
d. Incorrect. Asset tags are alpha coded by department.

4.

a. Correct. All departments are required to maintain records for any capital asset having a serial number.
b. Incorrect. Assets not subject to the city's capitalization policy are not required to be tagged.
c. Incorrect. Only assets that are not subject to the city's capitalization policy are not tagged.
d. Incorrect. Departments are required to maintain records for any capital asset having a serial number.

CHAPTER 8

Suggested Solutions to Case 8

1. The accountant could review day labor activity for selected or all locations. Names of day labor staff could be checked against the phone book, Facebook, Twitter, or some other reliable database or social networking website to determine if they are legitimate individuals.
2. Reviewing budget transfers from salaries to temporary payroll accounts may indicate a problem with dummy employees. Additionally, names of day labor staff could be checked against the phone book or some other reliable database to determine if they are legitimate individuals. Surprise visits could be conducted.
3. Traditional factors, such as low pay and long hours, contributed to the situations in this case. In addition, required minimum staffing levels put pressure on school program assistants to hire day labor in order to keep the programs running every day. The long lead time to hire and process new employees led to the day labor process which was used in this case to perpetrate fraud. In many cases, controls that are too onerous, or perceived as being such, may actually result in circumvention of them whether for fraudulent or mission-related purposes. It appears the HR and payroll compliance functions may be weak, as labor issues may exist with "day" labor.
4. Small amounts of misappropriated assets over a long period of time are not often detected by auditing procedures. Without a thorough and openly skeptical discussion of potential fraud risks, the auditor might never consider some areas as potential fraud risks. With respect to this situation, amounts paid to day laborers might not have been considered material in the aggregate in prior audits and therefore not subject to detail audit procedures.

Solutions to Knowledge Check Questions

1.

a. Correct. Students having scheduled tutoring sessions pay for tutoring services at the beginning of each week.
b. Incorrect. Most tutoring services are provided at 30 elementary and middle school libraries but some tutoring services are provided at the Smart Kids' office.
c. Incorrect. Amounts charged for tutoring services are based on household income.
d. Incorrect. Tutoring services are provided at the Smart Kids office as well as at 30 elementary and middle schools.

2.

a. Correct. Fred's wife is insisting she and Fred go through counseling.
b. Incorrect. There is no mention that Fred's children need braces for their teeth.
c. Incorrect. Fred has discussed his personal situation with two employees of Smart Kids.
d. Incorrect. Fred's personal situation has changed in the current year.

3.

a. Incorrect. Tim has been involved in his day laborer fraud schemes for some time.
b. Correct. Tim has four children and three ex-wives.
c. Incorrect. Tim voluntarily initiates a conversation with Fred regarding his day laborer fraud schemes.
d. Incorrect. Joe Francis told Tim the day laborer fraud schemes had been going on for years.

4.

a. Correct. Fred approaches Agnes Taylor about the day laborer fraud scheme.
b. Incorrect. The case does not mention that Fred has contacted local law enforcement about the day laborer fraud scheme.
c. Incorrect. The case does not mention that Fred has approached the board of directors about the day laborer fraud scheme.
d. Incorrect. Fred approaches Agnes Taylor about the day laborer fraud scheme.

CHAPTER 9

Suggested Solutions to Case 9

1. Purchases need to be reviewed by persons having the technical knowledge to determine the propriety and reasonableness of the purchase. In addition, management can develop financial and operational expectations and then compare them to actual results or situations and follow up on differences. For example, in this case a likely expectation about maintenance on a new helicopter might be that maintenance costs would be low or covered by a warranty. Typically, cross training helps to deter fraud, but in this case it is unlikely cross training would have been effective due to the highly technical aspects of helicopter operations and maintenance.
2. As part of the vendor set up process, accounts payable personnel could make a simple online inquiry using the vendor's name to determine if they exist or supply the types of goods and services appropriate to the entity or function, or both. Additionally, purchasing frequency reports might indicate purchasing patterns that are outside the norm or that are not consistent with management's expectations.
3. Originating department management should thoroughly review all vendors and purchases for propriety and reasonableness. When short-staffed or during peak service periods this is not always possible. Periodic training to remind operational personnel of the importance of internal controls, among other things, should be considered.
4. Using technology, vendor names and addresses can be matched against employee names and addresses as well as other external reliable databases. In detailed substantive tests or tests of controls, the auditor can determine if the purchase appears reasonable in light of the entity and the originating or benefiting function or department. Analytical procedures would also likely be an effective tool in detecting this situation.
5. Using either internal accounting or audit staff or external auditors, the sheriff should begin an investigation to determine whether fraud has occurred and to what extent. The investigation should cover at least the department in question and should probably be extended to other selected areas as well. The sheriff should, at a minimum, document the situation and what was done to date. The sheriff should also consult legal counsel to determine if the state Department of Law Enforcement should be notified and if so at what point. Additionally, the sheriff should discuss the situation with internal and external auditors and consider whether or not the county commission should be made aware of the situation. Other responses to this question will vary based on the experience and attitudes of participants.

Solutions to Knowledge Check Questions

1.

a. Incorrect. Bellview County is located in the northwest.
b. Incorrect. Bellview County is largely rural except for the County seat.
c. Correct. The majority of the residents of Bellview County are involved in the agricultural business.
d. Incorrect. Bellview County received a state grant to purchase its first helicopter.

2.

a. Correct. Black Widow is Bellview County's oldest helicopter.
b. Incorrect. King Cobra is Bellview County's newest helicopter.
c. Incorrect. The Bellview Sheriff's Department is responsible for the maintenance on King Cobra. The Bellview Fire Department is responsible for maintenance on Black Widow.
d. Incorrect. Bellview County currently owns two helicopters.

CHAPTER 10

Suggested Solutions to Case 10

1. Due to the limited number of staff, opportunity to misappropriate assets exists. The case does not mention any specific factors indicating employees have any incentive or feel any pressure that could lead them to commit fraud. Like other not-for-profit organizations, Central Clinic appears to operate with a limited amount of human, financial, and capital resources while offering a number of quality services to the community. These general conditions may result in increased fraud risks.
2. Controls over donated assets and capital assets are missing or ineffective. The director of finance is responsible for acknowledging donations. With the opportunity present in this case, having the director of finance acknowledge donated items could conceal misappropriated donated assets. Not conducting annual inventories of equipment provides staff with the opportunity to misappropriate physical assets. The fact that most assets are at the main clinic and would probably be missed does not adequately compensate for this missing control. There are a limited number of employees at the satellite clinic which may indicate controls could be missing or inadequate there.
3. Controls that could help minimize the potential for fraud include the following:
   - Tagging all fixed assets
   - Conducting annual inventories of physical assets
   - Acknowledgment of donated assets by someone other than the director of finance
   - Pre-employment high level background checks of all employees
   - Centralizing as many procedures as appropriate for the satellite clinic at the main clinic
   - Procedures to accept donations of equipment only on certain days or times and having donors sign a receipt for the specific items donated

4. Responses to this question will vary with the experience and attitudes of the participants. However, the discussion should be directed to discuss the following:
   - Obtain "page two" from County General and follow up as indicated and appropriate.
   - Determine if the lifestyle of the director of finance is commensurate with her income.
   - Investigate the lauras_secret_garden seller name and follow up as needed.

5. Preliminary audit procedures could include inquiries of staff as well as board members regarding the potential for or knowledge of fraud. Other audit procedures could include the following:
   - Confirmation of donated items using the letters of acknowledgement as well as ledger entries as a source
   - Physical inspection of assets (purchased and donated) using acknowledgment letters and the insurance schedule as a source
   - Tracing donated assets from acknowledgment letters to the insurance schedule or other fixed asset records
   - Tracing capital asset expenditures to the capital assets

Solutions to Knowledge Check Questions

1.

a. Correct. The board does not believe annual inventories of fixed assets are necessary because most equipment is housed at the main clinic.
b. Incorrect. The board believes assets included as "scheduled property" on the insurance policy should not be included in the asset identification system.
c. Incorrect. No asset identification system is used, as most capitalized items consist of equipment with serial numbers.
d. Incorrect. The director of finance sends a thank you letter meeting the requirements of the IRC to donors within 30 days of the donation.

2.

a. Correct. Central Clinic has a fixed asset policy which establishes a capitalization threshold for equipment at $2,500 and for buildings and improvements at $100,000.
b. Incorrect. In the case of donated equipment, senior management is responsible for obtaining information from donors regarding the estimated fair value of donated items.
c. Incorrect. Only a small amount of equipment is housed at the satellite clinic location.
d. Incorrect. Central Clinic uses various capitalization thresholds for various types of capital assets.

CHAPTER 11

Suggested Solutions to Case 11

1. Generally, the city's P-Card policies and procedures appear adequate, although they could have been expanded. In this case, the main problem was the issue of little or no oversight of the P-Card program. Periodic reviews of the various purchases, purchasers, and procedures might have discovered the fraud outlined in this case.
2. Because periodic oversight of the policies and procedures does not appear to have occurred or was ineffective, the city could have used technology to produce exception reports for purchase activity by vendor and purchases outside the normal purchasing cycle. In this case, the report would have shown an unusual level of activity for Kraft Supply based on purchases of prior periods.
3. The amounts purchased and misappropriated were small in nature and consistent in volume. They were also for items that could have been realistically used by the department and purchased from the vendor. Additionally, the same person was sent to purchase, pick up, and stock the legitimate purchases during this time. For these reasons, the fraud went undetected for almost a year. To prevent this type of fraud, someone could have phoned the order to the vendor and someone different could have been sent to pick it up. A review of all procurement card transactions by a

person having knowledge of the various departmental operations might also have prevented this type of fraud.

4. Audit procedures to test procurement card controls and activity could include the following:
   - Review of policies and procedures for adequacy
   - Review of compensating controls and procedures for adequacy
   - Inquiries of personnel regarding potential fraudulent procurement card transactions
   - Compliance tests of controls either separately for procurement card transactions or for any procurement card disbursement selected in general cash disbursements/ purchasing compliance tests
   - Substantive tests of details either separately for procurement card transactions or for any procurement card disbursement selected in general cash disbursements/ purchasing tests
   - Review of vendor activity levels for selected vendors
   - Analysis of the number and total amount of transactions per card, department, vendor, and so forth and comparison to prior year

Solutions to Knowledge Check Questions

1.

a. Incorrect. Accounts payable personnel review the P-Card statement for receipts that are attached.
b. Correct. Employees sign the P-Card statement indicating they have reviewed the purchases and are authorizing them for payment.
c. Incorrect. All employees being given P-Card privileges sign a P-Card authorization and agreement form.
d. Incorrect. Each employee assigned a P-Card is responsible for reconciling his or her monthly statement and attaching the receipts.

2.

a. Correct. An employee's immediate supervisor reviews the employee's P-Card statement and all related receipts.
b. Incorrect. The supervisor follows up with the employee if any receipts are missing or if any charges appear questionable.
c. Incorrect. An employee's immediate supervisor is required to review the employee's P-Card statement and all related receipts.
d. Incorrect. Accounts payable personnel review the P-Card statement for the proper signatures (employee and supervisor).

3.

a. Correct. The CFO reserves the right to review any P-Card statement activity at any time.
b. Incorrect. An exception report is electronically transmitted each day to the CFO.
c. Incorrect. All dollar and transaction limits, as well as allowable merchant codes, are programmed by the issuing financial institution into the card.
d. Incorrect. The P-Card authorization and agreement form is signed by employees being given P-Card privileges, their immediate supervisors, and their department directors.

CHAPTER 12

Suggested Solutions to Case 12

1. At a minimum, additional inquiries are necessary to determine the legitimacy of the noted overtime. The type and extent of additional procedures would depend on the resolution of the noted situations. If legitimate and reasonable, additional procedures may not be considered necessary. In some cases, even though the inquiries indicated the noted overtime was legitimate and reasonable, the auditor might want to review any items in the original sample in greater detail if overtime was paid for the selected item.
2. Responses to this question will vary based on the experience and attitudes of the participants. As presented, the items appear to possibly be fraud or abuse. There is insufficient information in the case to indicate whether or not management override occurred or if the fraud or abuse is material.

Solutions to Knowledge Check Questions

1.

a. Correct. The unemployment rate is high and individuals with a CDL are in high demand.
b. Incorrect. Helping Hands' mission is to provide transportation services between home and work, at no cost, to developmentally disabled adults.
c. Incorrect. The service area encompasses the three counties comprising the metropolitan area.
d. Incorrect. Helping Hands has been in existence for five years.

2.

a. Correct. The payroll clerk enters the information from the time sheet into the payroll system for processing.
b. Incorrect. Payroll department personnel ascertain that time sheets have been signed by the employee.
c. Incorrect. Payroll department personnel ascertain that time sheets have been signed by the employee's supervisor.
d. Incorrect. Overtime is not required to be approved by an employee's supervisor before it is worked.

3.

a. Incorrect. Payroll department personnel verify the math accuracy of each time sheet.
b. Correct. All overtime is to be approved by an employee's immediate supervisor.
c. Incorrect. Overtime is to be kept to a minimum and only incurred when it is necessary to provide services to Helping Hands' clients.
d. Incorrect. All overtime is to be approved by an employee's immediate supervisor.

Learn More

AICPA CPE

Thank you for selecting AICPA as your continuing professional education provider. We have a diverse offering of CPE courses to help you expand your skillset and develop your competencies. Choose from hundreds of different titles spanning the major subject matter areas relevant to CPAs and CGMAs, including:

- Governmental & Not-for-Profit accounting, auditing, and updates
- Internal control and fraud
- Audits of Employee Benefit Plans and 401(k) plans
- Individual and corporate tax updates
- A vast array of courses in other areas of accounting & auditing, controllership, management, consulting, taxation, and more!

Get your CPE when and where you want

- Self-study training options that includes on-demand, webcasts, and text formats with superior quality and a broad portfolio of topics, including bundled products like –
  - ➢ CPExpress for immediate access to hundreds of one and two-credit hour online courses for just-in-time learning at a price that is right
  - ➢ Annual Webcast Pass offering live Q&A with experts and unlimited access to the scheduled lineup, all at an incredible discount.
- Staff training programs for audit, tax and preparation, compilation and review
- Certificate programs offering comprehensive curriculums developed by practicing experts to build fundamental core competencies in specialized topics
- National conferences presented by recognized experts
- Affordable AICPA courses on-site at your organization – visit **aicpalearning.org/on-site** for more information.
- Seminars sponsored by your state society and led by top instructors. For a complete list, visit **aicpalearning.org/publicseminar**.

Take control of your career development

The AICPA I CIMA Competency and Learning website at **https://competency.aicpa.org** brings together a variety of learning resources and a self-assessment tool, enabling tracking and reporting of progress toward learning goals.

Visit the AICPA store at cpa2biz.com/CPE to browse our CPE selections.

Why AICPA?

Think of All the Great Reasons to Join the AICPA.

CAREER ADVOCACY SUPPORT
On behalf of the profession and public interest on the federal, state and local level.

PROFESSIONAL & PERSONAL DISCOUNTS
Save on travel, technology, office supplies, shipping and more.

ELEVATE YOUR CAREER
Five specialized credentials and designations (ABV®, CFF®, CITP®, PFS™ and CGMA®) enhance your value to clients and employers.

HELPING THE BEST AND THE BRIGHTEST
AICPA scholarships provide more than $350,000[1] to top accounting students.

GROW YOUR KNOWLEDGE
Discounted CPE on webcasts, self-study or on-demand courses & more than 60 specialized conferences & workshops.

PROFESSIONAL GUIDANCE YOU CAN COUNT ON
Technical hotlines & practice resources, including Ethics Hotline, Business & Industry Resource Center and the Financial Reporting Resource Center.

KEEPING YOU UP TO DATE
With news and publications from respected sources such as the *Journal of Accountancy*.

MAKING MEMBERS HAPPY
We maintain a 94%+ membership renewal rate.

FOUNDED ON INTEGRITY
Representing the profession for more than 125 years.

RELATIONSHIPS THAT COUNT
Over 400,000 Members in 145 Countries

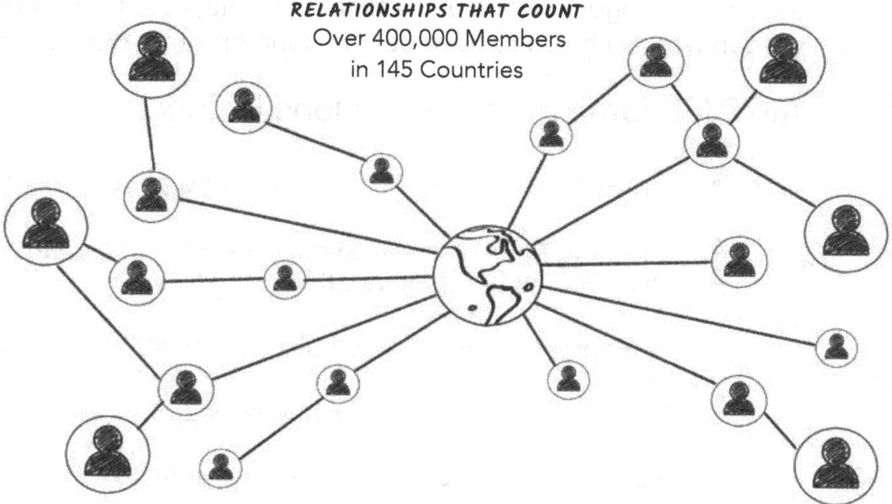

TO JOIN, VISIT:
aicpa.org/join or call 888.777.7077.

1. Source: AICPA Academic & Career Awareness